CITY WITH A CHANCE

City With a Chance

FRANK A. AUKOFER

THE BRUCE PUBLISHING COMPANY / MILWAUKEE

Library of Congress Catalog Card Number: 68–54077

To Sharlene,
who took care of everything else

INTRODUCTION

In the open housing demonstrations of 1967 that made Milwaukee famous, Negro children sang as they marched, "I just want to testify what the white man has done to me."

All over the United States in the summer of 1967 black people testified. In slum areas in northern cities — and a few in the south as well — windows crashed, bullets thudded into black and white flesh, and fires flared.

The implosions were of epidemic proportions, hopscotching from one city to another. They flared furiously but never quite died. They smolder still.

Implosions, rather than explosions, is the proper word to describe them. The riots that gutted the ghettos burst inward — not outward. The rage was visited on the very areas where it was spawned. The people who needed help were hurt.

Milwaukee, the city of beer, bratwurst, and gemütlichkeit; the stolid, conservative German of the midwest, was not spared. The tornado touched down there, too. There was hope that it would not happen, but the hope was tinged with knowledge that Milwaukee could have a riot, too — not in spite of what it was, but because of it.

Comparing cities, it has been said, is like comparing apples and oranges. True. Milwaukee is not Chicago, Chicago is not Detroit, Detroit is not Newark, Newark is not Watts. Each has its own peculiar characteristics, its history, ethnic composition, geography, climate, economy, and people.

Yet there were riots, and the riots were remarkably similar. The conditions that brought about those riots also were similar. Black men in Milwaukee rioted for the same reasons black men rioted in Newark and Detroit. The development of each city — how it arrived at the point where it attracted the destructive funnel cloud of a riot — differed not so much in kind as in degree. What was done and what was not done to stir black people into the great melting pot that America is supposed to be did not differ greatly from city to city.

The Negro in America has suffered, is suffering now, in Milwaukee as well as elsewhere. None but an ostrich could fail to see it. This is not to say that others are not suffering as well, particularly the poor of all colors — whites, American Indians, and Spanish-speaking Americans.

Yet Negroes have an identity no other group can claim. It is an identity of soul and skin color, of knowing one another as few others can know them, of knowing whites, in many cases, better than the whites know themselves, of being American longer than any migrant group, of knowing what it ought to mean to be an American, and yet not knowing it because of lack of experience with it.

Negroes in Milwaukee have this in common with Negroes in any city in the country. This is one reason why Milwaukee had a riot and why, for that matter, any city is susceptible.

What happened in Milwaukee and how it came about is the subject of this book. The details of its development, of course, it shares with no other city. But the basic causes of what happened in Milwaukee are the same as those in other cities.

Whitney M. Young, Jr., executive director of the National Urban League, is fond of saying that what is needed in this country to solve the "Negro problem" is more education — but the education, he says, must be directed at whites, not Negroes.

The story of Milwaukee might contribute, in a small way, to that educational process.

CONTENTS

CITY WITH A CHANCE

I

DETROIT CAME FIRST

July, 1967. We were in Detroit covering the riots. Buildings, their guts sucked out, still smoldered along Twelfth Street.

I had not been particularly anxious to go, even though riots in Negro ghettos were part of my beat as a civil rights reporter for *The Milwaukee Journal*.

There were two of us from the *Journal* on this one — the biggest ever. Kenneth C. Field was already there when I arrived, exhausted from working around the clock.

Neither of us made any attempt to cover the main story. The rioting was too widespread for a couple of out-of-town newspapermen, unfamiliar with the city, to try to compete on coverage with the well-staffed wire services.

We were there to cover the sidelights. In particular, my job was to probe the causes of the riots. So there was no pressing need for us to poke around in the riot areas themselves. But poke we did — it is difficult to keep any newspaperman from any place where things are happening.

We almost got our heads blown off. We will never know how close we came, but it was close enough to leave both of us shaking. And the threat came not from the rioters, but from the police.

We were driving around the city in a rented car one night after dark, not because we had any particular event to cover, but simply because we had to see the city during curfew time to get the feel of the situation.

Roadblocks manned by national guardsmen and police were everywhere. Streets were eerily vacant, save for an occasional police car or taxi speeding past with its lights out. No lights, no target — or so they hoped. There had been reports of snipers everywhere.

We encountered little difficulty at the roadblocks until we neared the main riot area where the command post for police and national guardsmen had been set up. We could hear gunfire — single shots and staccato bursts from automatic weapons.

Crossing a bridge over the John C. Lodge Freeway, we encountered guardsmen and police huddled next to their jeeps and squad cars, peering up at an apartment building with rifles, automatic weapons, and pistols at the ready.

Field, fresh from covering the Newark riots, sensed immediately what was happening and slid down in his seat.

A sniper!

I was driving. I had nowhere to hide. It was the first time I had ever felt so exposed sitting inside an automobile. A guardsman walked up.

"Press," I said, holding out my identification card.

"Get the hell out of here," he snarled. "And douse those lights."

I did not need a second invitation. I made a quick left turn and gunned the Ford hardtop down a frontage road next to the freeway. The road was the western boundary of the area from which most of the sniper reports had come that night.

A few blocks down, I eased off on the accelerator. The street was deserted. We started looking for a way out of the area. Then we saw the car.

It was a big, battered old Chrysler, maybe a 1957 or 1958 model, sitting silently near the left curb. My right foot involuntarily lifted off the pedal, and the Ford slowed to a crawl.

As we came up on the car, a middle-aged Negro man opened the right door, climbed out and walked toward us. He started talking rapidly — we did not understand most of it, but caught enough to know that his car had conked out.

Then two others got out of the car — another middle-aged Negro man and a young Negro woman carrying a crying child about 16 months old. The woman was crying, too — hysterically — and waving a piece of paper.

The three of them were all talking at once, while we sat rigid in the car. It seemed that the woman had taken her sick baby to a hospital — the piece of paper was an outpatient form and she showed it to us to prove she was telling the truth.

She had been caught on the streets after the curfew and the two men in the car had given her a ride. Then the car stalled. I had never before seen anyone so frightened. Could we help them out of there?

We could, I said, reaching around to unlock the back door. What else was there for us to do? We were, at that point, frightened, too. But we could not leave them there to maybe be shot as snipers.

Field started yelling, "Press! Press!" I looked over and saw him waving his press card out the right window. Then I glanced in the rear view mirror.

There, behind us, were two police cruisers and perhaps 15 policemen on foot, advancing slowly on our car, their rifles and shotguns pointed directly at us. I started yelling, too, and opened the door to get out. Half a dozen of the policemen dropped to one knee, their weapons pointed at me.

As quickly as I dared, I walked to the nearest police officer. There seemed to be no one in particular in command. I explained the situation to him. He never looked at me once. He looked at my press card, then watched the car while I talked.

Finally, he said, "All right. But back it out of here. There's snipers in there."

Relieved, I walked rapidly back to the car. By this time, the other policemen had formed a semicircle around the car, but well away from it.

The two Negro men in the back seat sat stiffly, staring straight ahead. The woman, still crying, rocked back and forth in the seat, hugging her feverish baby to her chest. Her right hand still clutched the outpatient form. Field, who is a Negro — all the policemen were white — was hunched down in his seat.

I put the car in gear and started backing up.

"Where the hell you going!" The shout was a demand, not a question. Three policemen on my left were pointing their rifles at the car.

"I'm backing up," I yelled. "The guy over there told me to back up."

The rifles, pointed from the hip, went up to their shoulders.

"Get the hell out of here!" one of them yelled. "You sonsabitches don't belong here anyway. Get your goddam asses out of here! They're killing cops all over here!"

I fumbled for the shift lever, missed the slot, then finally clicked it into drive. The car lurched forward. I stood on the accelerator pedal until we were well away.

We drove slowly, tentatively after that, avoiding police cars and road blocks. We managed to get back across the Lodge Freeway, away from the main sniper area. The woman lived in the area. Getting her home was out of the question. One of the two men lived about a block outside the area.

We finally managed to pick our way through the streets to a point about a half block from his house. The woman and the other man would spend the night there.

Her terror had subsided somewhat and now she was concerned about her husband. How would she tell him she was all right? The man apologized. He had no telephone. There was nothing she could do but wait out the night and hope that her husband did not go out on the streets looking for her.

There was nothing more Field and I could do, either, except wish them luck. As we were leaving one of the men leaned toward the window on my side of the car, very slowly told me his name and address, and thanked us.

"If you ever need anything — anything at all," he said, "you come on over. You saved our lives."

Against the backdrop of the fires, killing, and looting of the worst Negro ghetto riot in history, the incident was insignificant. Neither Field nor I ever wrote anything about it. Many reporters, including ourselves, have had experiences covering assignments more harrowing than that brief encounter.

I only relate it here to illustrate, in a small way, what happens to a large northern city gripped by a riot. The four Negroes — the two men, the woman, and the baby — were faces in the night, people no one ever heard of, people no one ever is likely to hear about again.

Yet they were human beings, terrorized by something that was neither of their choosing nor their making. They were Negroes who happened to be living in an area where there was what some called a Negro riot. There were thousands of others like them — huddled, frightened, in their homes, afraid not only of the riot itself but of being mistaken, because of their black skins, for one of the rioters.

But the fear was not one-sided. The policemen who so frightened us were afraid themselves — afraid of being shot by an unseen sniper, afraid because of the rumors that circulated, because of the reports — many false — that came in over their radios. Their reaction to six harmless people showed their fear.

"They" were not "killing cops all over down there." There were a few incidents that night, but the official report later was that it had been comparatively quiet.

Detroit suffered. Her people, black and white, suffered with her. Millions of words have told how they suffered because of the modern urban phenomenon of the ghetto riot.

We steered clear of the riot areas after that. I spent the rest of my time interviewing all the people I could find who might be able to shed some light on the causes of the riot and also on how Detroit compared to my own city, Milwaukee.

Milwaukeeans, too, feared a riot. They were not alone. People in big cities all over the country in the summer of 1967 feared the same thing. Yet even though the fear was present, there were many in Milwaukee who were betting that it would not follow in the pattern of other cities.

Milwaukee was too good a city, they said. It had problems, to be sure, but they were not the problems of a Newark, a Detroit, or a Watts. Milwaukee had a fine reputation as a solid, somewhat conservative city, a good place in which to raise a family. A fine police force. Slums, yes, but not as slummy as in many other cities.

Detroiters had said the same things, and had said them with even more conviction. It had a terrible race riot once, in 1943, and this had awakened its citizens to the problems of the Negro minority and the poor.

As I went about my interviews, I learned that, in many ways, Detroit had been doing many more things than Milwaukee that could be considered as preventive maintenance against a riot. I started working on a story comparing the efforts of the two cities.

Each day, as I worked out of the city room of *The Detroit News,* the reports were coming in. Riots in Flint, South Bend, Chicago. I waited for the word that would send me flying back to Milwaukee to cover a riot in my home town, perhaps in the inner city neighborhood where I was born.

It did not come while I was in Detroit. Relieved, I returned home, thinking that maybe — just maybe — Milwaukee might slip through the summer without being added to the list.

Yet I knew that it was just wishful thinking, that if Milwaukee did manage to get through the summer without a riot, it would be pure luck. The story I was working on would show that.

The story appeared on the front page of *The Milwaukee Journal* on Sunday, July 30. Datelined Detroit, it began: "If there is a lesson for Milwaukee from the riots here last week, it is that the best is not good enough."

The story went on to point out that Detroit had been a model of what could be done about race relations and the problems of the poor, how Detroit had been called the "best in the nation" in these matters.

I compared the cities themselves, their racial and geographic characteristics, the civil rights issues they had faced, and the programs they had inaugurated to alleviate the problems of the poor and the ghetto Negro. In almost every case, the story showed that Detroit had done more than Milwaukee, partly because it was a bigger city with bigger problems, but also because it had, in some cases, been more forward-looking.

Reading my own story that Sunday, I thought — somewhat unrealistically — that maybe the story might awaken some people in Milwaukee to the fact that the city had to do more, much more, if it wanted to avoid the destruction that Detroit had experienced.

That night, I took my wife and children to a drive-in movie. We returned home about 1 a.m.

Not more than an hour later, the telephone rang. I stumbled sleepily out of bed and answered it. It was the assistant city editor of the *Journal*.

Milwaukee had a riot.

II
MILWAUKEE JOINS THE LIST

Mayor Henry W. Maier called it a civil disturbance. The newspapers headlined it as a Negro riot. Father James E. Groppi called it a revolution. For economy, and for no other reason, it will be referred to here simply as a riot.

However you view it, it locked up the city of Milwaukee and much of the metropolitan area for nearly nine and a half days. Nothing had ever so staggered the city before.

From a statistical standpoint, it was not much of a riot compared to others in the summer of 1967. Milwaukee's riot left three persons dead of gunshot wounds — one of them an accidental shooting — about 100 persons injured, including 44 policemen, and 1,740 persons arrested. Most of the arrests were for violation of the mayor's tight curfew, which was widely credited with keeping the lid from blowing off.

Compared to Detroit, the Milwaukee riot was a puff of smoke. Forty-three were killed, nearly 2,000 were injured, and more than 7,000 persons were arrested in the Motor City. Newark, too, had a worse time with 23 dead, more than 1,000 injured, and about 1,400 arrests.

Although the curfew and other restrictions in Milwaukee lasted nearly ten days, the riot itself was mostly confined to a five-hour period the night of July 30–31, from 9:45 p.m. to 2:45 a.m.

It started on Milwaukee's North Third Street. Third Street is one

7

of those dilapidated business arteries that can be found in the Negro ghettos of almost any modern northern city. Once it had been a thriving area for businesses and retail stores — before the days of the shopping centers, people from all over the city had gone to Third Street to shop.

By July 30, 1967, the street had become an area populated mostly by discount stores, taverns, small grocery stores, barber shops, shoe shine parlors — even a Black Muslim temple. One large department store — Gimbels-Schusters — which had been there in the heydey of the street, remained to remind people that Third Street had once been proud. Also on Third Street were many of the offices of organizations and agencies which provide service to the slum dwellers. In short, Third Street was Main Street for Milwaukee's Negro community.

Sunday night, July 30, was one of those warm summer nights that brings slum dwellers out on the streets. The atmosphere was made warmer by widespread rumors, in and out of the Negro community, that Milwaukee was due for a riot. The Detroit riot was fresh in everyone's mind, and there had been an incident on Third Street early Sunday morning, 18 hours before the riot started.

As with so many incidents witnessed only by the people involved in them and by the police, details never become quite clear. The police said it started outside The Scene, a downtown night club. Two Negro women were fighting on the sidewalk and a crowd of about 350 persons — black and white — gathered to watch.

When the police moved in to break up the fight, bottles and other missiles flew at them from the crowd. They called for reinforcements. Most of the whites left quickly, but the Negroes were more adamant. Police prodded them and moved the crowd north on Third Street. The crowd moved 15 blocks before it broke up completely.

The daylight hours on Sunday were uneventful. But by 9 p.m. the street was alive with people, most of them young Negroes.

Other riots had incidents that touched them off. In Detroit, for example, police raided five after-hours drinking spots — "blind pigs" — and after the fifth raid rumors of police brutality shot through the neighborhood.

But in Milwaukee there seemed to be no such spark, although some Negroes claimed afterward that what triggered the events was when police broke up a crowd of Negro youths who had attended a dance Sunday evening.

The first report of violence reached police headquarters about 9:45 p.m. Negroes, it said, had broken windows at a Third Street intersection. The situation soon went out of control. Youths in cars drove around the area honking horns. Bands of young Negroes — police later estimated the total number at about 300 — roved up and down Third Street and on adjacent streets. Bottles, stones, cans, and chunks of concrete were thrown at passing cars. Hundreds of windows were broken.

Surprisingly, there was little looting.

At 11:43 p.m., police notified the mayor of the disturbance. Two minutes later, Mayor Maier alerted Wisconsin Governor Warren P. Knowles. By 12:10 a.m., the mayor was in city hall. Half an hour later, he called the governor and asked him to put the Red Arrow Division, Wisconsin National Guard, on alert.

Repeated outbreaks of small fires prompted Fire Chief James R. Moher to call the mayor at 1 a.m. Fifty minutes later, he called back again and asked for national guard troops.

The mayor held off for 36 minutes — until Police Chief Harold A. Breier, who had set up a command post in the area, also asked for the guard. Two minutes later, Mayor Maier was on his "hot line" to the governor. At the same time, the mayor declared a state of emergency, coupled with a 24-hour curfew. He also notified the White House in Washington — a hedge against the possible need to request federal troops.

Maier later said he had known that the riot was coming and had been prepared for it — installation of the hot line was one example. He said he was surprised that it had not happened sooner. Milwaukee was bound to have a riot, he said, because riots had become a form of contagion around the country.

The mayor said he was convinced that the riot was not motivated by civil rights. Many Negroes would disagree. But he laid part of the blame on what he called "so-called civil rights leaders who have been encouraging defiance of the law." He would not name any names, but it was obvious that Father Groppi's was one of them.

Henry W. Maier, 50, had been mayor of Milwaukee since 1960, when he came from behind to defeat a Milwaukee congressman, Henry S. Reuss. A strong man in a weak mayor system of government, he had the ability to inspire total loyalty or bitter alienation in various Milwaukeeans. He was a student of municipal government, an astute politician, and a top administrator.

But he was also autocratic in outlook, with a "Henry knows best" attitude. As a result, he was often supersensitive to criticism, particularly to criticism by newspaper editorial writers.

Although he often emphasized the need for communications in running the city, Henry Maier's communication with most of the established Negro leadership in Milwaukee was almost nil. An established and highly respected member of the Negro community, who was not a civil rights activist in any sense of the term, put it this way: "The mayor has always felt that those people in that neck of the woods, as he puts it, didn't put him in office and he owes no allegiance to them."

The worst incident related to Milwaukee's riot was unfolding early Monday morning, July 31, as the mayor was requesting national guard troops for the city.

The first police call, inaccurate in the confusion of the night, said: "Send ambulance. One dead already. Send ambulance. 134 West Center. Man shot in head by sniper."

As it turned out, there were two dead in the house. But no one learned about them until long after the first call at 2:03 a.m. The bodies of Patrolman Bryan Moschea, 24, and Mrs. Anne Mosley, 77, were found in the ruins of the burned-out home. Moschea was killed by a blast from a shotgun; Mrs. Mosley had been shot in the head.

Six policemen were wounded, also by shotgun blasts, and a seventh was cut by flying glass shattered when he narrowly missed getting shot. One of the wounded policemen, 25-year-old John Carter, was permanently blinded. A detective captain, Kenneth J. Hagopian, 41, had part of his face shot away.

John Oraa Tucker, 55 years old, Negro, and a trusted janitor at suburban Shorewood High School, later was charged with the murder of Moschea and nine counts of attempted murder for shooting at the other policemen.

Tucker had been home with his wife, Mrs. Willie Olivia Tucker, 55, when the riot started on Third Street. "They was throwing bricks and making a racket," Mrs. Tucker said later. "I couldn't sleep. Then there was gunfire and tear gas and fire."

Tucker and his wife were babysitting with their grandson's two children, five and six years old. The grandson, Lessie D. Nichols, 23, went to the home about 1:15 or 1:30 a.m. to pick them up. A group of neighbors stood on the sidewalk, talking. Nichols joined them.

A white man in a white station wagon passed by and, Nichols said, shouted profanities at the group on the sidewalk. Tucker also told of the white man in the car. He said the man called him a "black nigger" and threatened to kill him and the others. A neighbor, Mrs. Hannah Jackson, 23, who was wounded with shotgun pellets during the incident, said the man in the car had shot at her.

Tucker testified in his trial that he was afraid the man was going to kill all of them. He said he went inside his house, got his shotgun and came back outside. The white man shot at him, he said, and he fired back. Then, he testified, another car pulled up and a man jumped out. "I fired at him," Tucker said.

The second man, according to witnesses, was Hagopian. He had arrived at the scene in an unmarked police car with four other plain-clothes detectives. The car had responded to a call at 1:59 a.m. to investigate a report of a man shooting from a car in an area about four blocks east of the Tucker home. When the officers arrived, they found nothing, so they cruised west toward Tucker's house.

They saw Tucker standing near his home with a shotgun, according to one of the detectives. Tucker started firing when the detectives stopped their car and started getting out, they said.

Moschea was among the reinforcements that arrived. He was the first policeman to go into the house. As he stood in the darkened living room, a shotgun roared. The birdshot hit him in the chest and throat. Another patrolman who was shot near Moschea managed to stagger out of the house. Carter also was shot inside the house.

But Tucker testified that he did not shoot at anyone who was inside the house. He said he shot only once while he was inside, through a window toward the outside. After firing the shot, he said, he hid the shotgun, went outside and surrendered.

Police lobbed tear gas grenades into the house. One of the smoldering grenades started a fire that left the house in ruins. The bodies of Mrs. Mosley and Moschea were found in the burned-out building. The Milwaukee county medical examiner's office later received a report from the police department saying that Mrs. Mosley had been shot accidentally during the incident. Tucker eventually was acquitted on Moschea's murder and three of the nine attempted murder charges. However, he was convicted of six counts of endangering safety by conduct regardless of life.

Meanwhile, Police Chief Breier had set up the command post at the Gimbels-Schusters garage. Slowly, the more than 1,000 police on duty quelled the rioting bands. A gentle rain started falling at about 2:45 a.m. and no doubt helped get people off the streets.

At daybreak, Milwaukee was a ghost town. Suburban police departments had set up roadblocks on major highways leading into the city. Milwaukee police also had squad cars and riot armed men at major intersections around the riot area.

Two persons were dead, at least 70 had been injured and 180 persons were under arrest. Early arrests were for burglary, theft, attempted arson, and criminal damage to property. As the days wore on, more persons were arrested, but the arrests mostly were for violation of the mayor's strict curfew.

By Monday morning, 450 national guardsmen were on duty in the city, with another 1,000 standing by at staging areas. The number swelled to 4,800 by midnight as guardsmen poured in from around the state.

They had little to do. Their presence, coupled with the strict curfew, apparently kept further rioting from breaking out. There were other incidents in the succeeding days, but for all practical purposes, the riot had reached its peak and died during that five-hour period Sunday night and early Monday.

One more death was yet to be recorded, however. It was a death that sickened and angered Milwaukee's Negroes. As this is written, no clear story has yet emerged of what happened that Wednesday night, August 2.

One thing is clear. Clifford McKissick, 18 years old, a college student and one of nine children, died that night of a police bullet through the neck. The police said that McKissick and three other youths had tried to set fire to a paint store across the alley from his home with molotov cocktails — bottles filled with gasoline. He was shot while fleeing from policemen who had been staked out near the store, according to the police accounts.

McKissick's family and several neighbors, however, said that Clifford had been sitting on the front porch when they all heard shooting. Everyone ran — no one saw exactly where McKissick headed — and a few minutes later he stumbled into the back door of the home, choking from the bullet through his throat.

His death was ruled justifiable homicide. Whether it was may never be known, and that is tragic. It is tragic because of the effect it had on the Negro community. To many Milwaukee Negroes, McKissick's death was simply another case of a white man killing a nigger and getting away with it.

An example of some of the Negro reaction came several weeks later. A Negro painter had announced that he was establishing a fund for the McKissick family. He called a meeting at the inner city YMCA in connection with the fund, but only about ten persons, all of them young Negro men, showed up. It may be that there was a lack of interest in the meeting, or in the man who called it, or perhaps the meeting simply was not widely enough publicized.

Also at the meeting were two plain-clothes detectives, there at the invitation of the man who had called the meeting. They sat at the side of the room and the Negroes present knew that they were policemen. Yet that did not stop them from voicing their rage at the killing of McKissick and their hatred of policemen in general.

Four of the young men were particularly volatile. To them, McKissick's death was the last straw. They were ex-servicemen, they said, who had served their country, two of them in the marine corps. They had returned from service only to be forced to live in Milwaukee's inner core, the slummiest area of the city. And they hated cops.

Several of them said that they were not going to take any more. They were tired of white policemen watching them, hounding them, treating them as if they were criminals whether they did something wrong or not. And they were at the point, they said, where they would no longer retaliate by fighting with their fists.

"The next time a cop stops my wife on the street and yells at her, 'Hey, girl, where you going?' I'm going to kill him," one said. "I'm not just going to beat him up, I'm going to kill him."

Their main contention was not a charge of police brutality, although one of them did relate an incident in which policemen arrested him on suspicion of robbery and allegedly threatened to kill him. Mostly, they were upset about the general attitude of the police in Milwaukee's inner city as they saw it.

The point, as another put it, was that policemen in the inner city were always *watching* the people, while in the suburbs and white areas of the city, police *protected* the people.

Policemen would argue that they have to be watchful in any ghetto area, where there is a high rate of crime. This is no doubt true, but it still does not alter the fact that policemen, to many ghetto dwellers, symbolize the oppression they suffer at the hands of white society. The policeman — as a concept, not necessarily as an individual — is probably the most hated entity in any Negro ghetto. "To many Negroes," said the US Advisory Commission on Civil Disorders, "police have come to symbolize white power, white racism and white repression." Yet individually, some policemen, black and white, have good relationships with people in the ghetto. And, incongruously, the first thing many ghetto dwellers do when trouble starts is to call the police.

Even if the police were fully justified in shooting young McKissick, even if a full public inquiry proved it, some Negroes still would harbor doubt and add it to their personal list of grievances. The fact that doubt remained in the case just made it more convincing to the people who viewed it as another incident of police oppression.

Whether this is unreasonable and illogical depends on one's viewpoint. To the average white suburbanite whose only experience with the police is buying bicycle licenses or having his house checked while the family is off camping, it is unreasonable. But to the ghetto dweller who has been stopped and questioned on the street while doing nothing more than going to the corner grocery store, it is not.

And this sort of "illogical" thinking is not exclusive in Negro neighborhoods. Anyone who has ever attended a village board session, common council hearing, or school tax meeting can testify to this. People always are most concerned with what affects them most directly. If the snow in front of my house is not plowed before I leave for work at 7 o'clock in the morning, all the logical statements in the world about the efficiency of the way the city's streets are scheduled for plowing will not sway me from arguing vehemently that I want the city to plow my street earlier.

Similarly, civic leaders, churchmen, and editorial writers can argue logically and reasonably for the passage of an open housing law, as they did in Milwaukee, but it doesn't mean beans to the white man whose worst fear is that his daughter might meet, fall in love with, and maybe marry a Negro.

So McKissick's death, to some Milwaukee Negroes, was another piece of sandpaper grating away at them.

The night after McKissick's death was the quietest since the Sunday night-early Monday riot. It prompted Mayor Maier to relax the curfew and permit beer and liquor sales to resume. By Saturday,

August 5, the riot and subsequent events were no longer the top story in *The Milwaukee Journal*. At 5 a.m. Wednesday, August 9, the curfew and the city's state of emergency were over.

The mayor was widely hailed everywhere but in Milwaukee's black community for his tactics in snuffing out the riot. His reaction was swift and effective — a total curfew, closing of all taverns, liquor stores, and service stations in the city, and national guard troops in the city within hours to back up the police.

The mayor, or course, was reacting to a notion of what might have happened as well as to what actually did happen. The entire country, as a result of Newark and Detroit, had been conditioned on what to expect. Mayor Maier was no exception.

Yet it was difficult to fault his conduct in putting down the riot. Even some of his most ardent detractors admitted to a twinge of admiration for the mayor in the days following the riot when the city was breathing a little easier again. Whether it was necessary to keep the curfew on for nearly ten days is another matter.

Detroit officials were criticized for not reacting quickly enough. There could be no such criticism of Milwaukee.

No one, of course, knows what would have happened if the mayor had reacted differently. As noted earlier, the riot itself was not much as modern urban riots go, although President Johnson's riot commission did classify it as one of eight major disorders during the summer. Maier himself pointed out that only two-tenths of one percent of Milwaukee's 90,000 Negroes had been involved in the rioting. Police, without the assistance of the national guard, had the situation under control five hours after it started.

There were only two serious fires in the inner core that night, one of them at the Tucker home, and there was far less looting than in other cities. Take away the two deaths and the wounding of six policemen at the Tucker home — in another part of the city or at another time, it would have been recorded simply as a shooting incident — and Milwaukee's riot was largely teen-age vandalism.

The Tucker incident was, of course, part of the riot, but more because of circumstances than any outright desire to participate. As nearly as can be determined at this point, Tucker reacted out of fear, not anger or any predetermined desire to get whitey.

There were other incidents in the nights after the riot, but for the most part police spent their time chasing down false reports. The death of McKissick was the worst incident. There also was some sniper activity reported, but the total number of shots fired by snipers probably would not have filled one patrolman's cartridge belt.

One tense incident occurred Monday afternoon, July 31, less than 12 hours after police had the riot under control, when Father Groppi and seven members of the Milwaukee NAACP Youth Council were arrested for violation of the mayor's curfew. The priest explained that he and the others were on their way to a meeting of Negro community leaders at Northcott Neighborhood House, a Methodist agency in the inner core. In a stated desire to keep the arrests from sparking further violence, Mayor Maier sent a representative to assure that Father Groppi and the others were processed through court quickly. All of them were released without bail.

Joseph C. Fagan, chairman of the Wisconsin Department of Industry, Labor and Human Relations, had issued letters for Father Groppi and other civil rights leaders to assist them in getting through police lines. The letters had no official standing, but Fagan hoped they would serve as identification and help the civil rights leaders move about to help calm the situation. Fagan, a Republican appointed to his post by Governor Knowles, had surprised many by his continuing efforts to establish communications and to work with community leaders and residents of the inner core.

His work in this area had frequently brought him in conflict with the mayor, who viewed Fagan as a political enemy. The letters did not lessen it. In a blistering statement, Mayor Maier accused Fagan of acting like a "curbstone commissar." He asked the state attorney general to investigate whether legal action could be taken against Fagan. But the issue never went beyond the flurry of public statements.

The riot, meanwhile, produced an unusual incident of black solidarity in Milwaukee. A group of Negro community leaders, representatives of inner city organizations, and so-called "grass roots" people began meeting quietly behind closed doors. The situation was unusual because the participants represented a broad cross section of the black community — people off the streets, civil rights militants, and even men who in the past had been referred to as "Uncle Toms."

After a meeting on Tuesday, August 1, the new organization, which called itself the Common View Group, issued a statement charging Milwaukee's "white power structure" with major responsibility for the riot. "The paternalistic attitude of the white power structure, in 'knowing' all of the answers as to what is best for the black community has been the major contributing factor which led to the present confrontation," the statement said.

The statement included a long list of grievances in the areas of education, housing, employment, and police-community relations. It accused the mayor and city government of avoiding the need for improvement in these areas, and said the white power structure was ignoring the need for communication with the city's Negro community.

Several members of the group claimed that they had been re-buffed when they offered their help. Paul J. Moynihan, chairman of the city's Commission on Community Relations, bristled. "This thing about not trying to establish meaningful communications," he said, "is absolute nonsense." He said he and other representatives of the mayor's office had made a continuous effort to reach all representatives of the Negro community for their help in the situation.

In an attempt to close the breach, Jules Modlinski, a Marquette University official who had worked with inner core agencies during the summer on a youth employment program, called Negro community leaders and set up a meeting at the inner core YMCA. Moynihan went to the meeting with Calvin W. Beckett, executive secretary of the Community Relations Commission. The commission was Milwaukee's official — and heretofore mostly inept — agency in the human rights field.

The meeting fizzled before it ever got underway. Some community leaders and inner city residents who attended had expected the mayor. When he did not show up, many of them drowned out Moynihan with shouting and walked out. Modlinski conceded that Mayor Maier had not been promised, but also contended that the mayor should have recognized existing leadership in the inner core.

Mayor Maier did meet with a group from the inner core, but it was a meeting that angered many of the civil rights leaders, agency representatives, and other members of the Common View Group. The meeting, held on Friday, August 4, at the mayor's invitation, was with 47 Negroes whom Maier called the "grass roots Negro leaders" — ministers, union stewards, bartenders, barbers, and other businessmen.

". . . And porters, swampers and janitors," one black leader said in referring to the meeting. Many members of the Common View Group were furious because, in their view, the mayor was setting himself up as the judge of who Milwaukee's Negro leaders were. And, they believed, he was judging on the basis of his personal stereotypes.

There was criticism from other fronts, too. A group of whites and Negroes who represented moderate and militant civil rights viewpoints had met the day before and agreed that the mayor was attempting to bypass organizations that served the inner core. Among those at the meeting were a labor leader, welfare and antipoverty program officials, and the executive director of Milwaukee's United Community Services.

At the meeting, there also was criticism of a proposal made earlier by Mayor Maier to establish "a new kind of biracial committee." Corneff Taylor, research director for the Milwaukee Urban League and former executive secretary of the Community Relations Commission, said: "He's up to his old tricks of appointing a new committee whenever he finds himself in a situation that needs immediate attention."

The mayor met with another group on Saturday, August 5 — this time with members of the Interdenominational Ministerial Alliance, an organization of Negro clergymen. After the meeting, Maier announced a Thirty-Nine Point Program, which was heralded as an assault on the city's racial problems.

Many of the points were similar or identical to earlier proposals the mayor had made in his continuing campaign for more state and federal help for the city. Most of the points led off with the words, "That the mayor seek," "That the county furnish," "That there be a federal program," "That the state establish," and other similar phrases directed at other levels of government. Most of them required little more than advocacy from the mayor, and he had advocated them before.

The Common View Group also came up with a series of proposals, covering 30 points under six headings — housing, employment, education, police-community relations, the court system, and recreation. Its proposals were in a statement that reflected moderation. The statement supported Maier's efforts to get increased financial aid for the city, and applauded his efforts to strengthen the office of the mayor of Milwaukee. The Common View members said they would use the resources of their group to help the mayor realize these goals.

But the 30 points of the Common View Group concentrated on

actions its members believed the mayor could take, while the mayor's 39 points concentrated on measures by other levels of government.

Although the mayor finally did meet with the Common View Group later, there never was a meeting of the minds. Maier went on talking about his thirty-nine points, and the Common View Group withered away and was not heard from again.

For some time before the riot struck Milwaukee, close advisers to Milwaukee's Catholic Archbishop, William E. Cousins, had been urging him to make a major address on civil rights. Although the archbishop was firmly committed to the cause — he had, for example, resisted powerful pressures to have him take action against Father Groppi — his beliefs had been largely locked behind closed doors.

Cousins, 64, had been archbishop of Milwaukee since December, 1958. A genial, outgoing man, he had become quite popular with the majority of the Milwaukee area's Catholics. But with the advent of the civil rights movement in Milwaukee, he was shot at from both sides. Liberals wanted him to be more outspoken and involved in civil rights matters, while conservatives badgered him to muzzle Father Groppi.

The major civil rights speech finally came on August 6, exactly a week after the riot broke out. Speaking over nine radio and four television stations to the nearly 700,000 Catholics in the Milwaukee area, the archbishop deplored rioting and lawlessness, but said they called attention to problems that could not be ignored. He also said that Catholics had a sacred duty to free their communities of racial prejudice.

Archbishop Cousins spoke strictly as a churchman and strictly to Catholics. He did not outline any specific programs, saying that others besides the Church also had to help solve the problems, including all levels of government, industry and labor, and the communications media.

Without mentioning Father Groppi by name, the archbishop defended the participation of priests and nuns in civil rights demonstrations. "They are not the cause of unrest," he said. "They are not responsible for existing conditions. If they were to withdraw completely from the scene, our minority and racial problems would still be with us. A swinging red light at a railroad crossing doesn't create the danger; it simply calls attention to it."

Two days later, the mayor went before the television cameras in a major speech that marked the end of the state of emergency caused by the riot. "Never was there a more important time," he said, "for everyone to get together with understanding to build a better city. I think it would be tragic if we decided that the answer is a bigger and better billy club."

Maier reiterated his often-repeated conclusion that the city of Milwaukee needed more help from other units of government. "The central city of Milwaukee," he said, "can no more finance the crucial problems of poverty, ignorance, disease and discrimination with the property taxes of relatively poor people than the city of Milwaukee can finance sending a man to the moon."

He also made a plea for racial harmony. He said that although the rioters were mostly nonwhite, "it must be remembered that the overwhelming percentage of nonwhites, like the overwhelming percentage of all whites, are concerned about the safety of their neighborhoods, the quality of their homes, the education of their children and the chance for a good job. The guilty deserve to be punished. They must feel the full penalty of the law. But the majority should not suffer for the deeds of a criminal few."

It was a statesmanlike speech, calculated to soothe the city. Maier came through the riot and the state of emergency with his stock higher than it ever had been. Some of the civil rights leaders were not impressed. Said one: "It's really nothing but a mishmash of his past abdication of leadership by passing the buck on to other levels of government." But nobody was listening to the civil rights leaders.

As Mayor Maier pointed out, the vast majority of Milwaukee's black citizens were not involved in the riot, harassment of police, or sniper activity. No more than 300 persons participated. Yet they tied up a metropolitan area and directly affected the lives of nearly 1.4 million people. The costs, in relation to the number of people actually involved, were staggering. Property damage alone totaled more than a half million dollars. Overtime for police and firemen, the cost of calling out the national guard, and the time lost by people who could not get to work represented uncounted dollars that never could be recovered.

Yet there were many among those 1.4 million people who, if asked, would not have authorized the spending of a fraction of that money on preventive maintenance against another such occurrence. More often than not, the cry was for increased repression instead of money to cure the problems that caused the riot in the first place.

III

NO SIMPLE ANSWERS

In the weeks following the Milwaukee riot, about half a dozen letters came to my desk in the *Journal* newsroom accusing me of starting the riot because of the story I had written comparing Milwaukee and Detroit. I thought it unusual that even that many people considered the printed word so powerful that it could, by itself, set off a riot.

The story was a coincidence, nothing more. But the letters I received showed the way many people cast about for simple explanations and scapegoats. Disasters of any kind seldom, if ever, have a single, simple cause. A one-car accident in which the driver is killed might look like the sort of disaster that could have a simple explanation. The driver was speeding, lost control of the car, went off the road, and struck a tree.

Yet studies have shown that such accidents are not so simple. Perhaps the driver had been drinking, or taking medicine, or was tired, or worried about his job or his wife and family, or perhaps he sneezed at just the wrong moment, or maybe a bee flew in the window. Perhaps a tire blew, or the brakes locked, or a leaky muffler made the driver sleepy from carbon monoxide, or a tie rod in the front end broke, or a shock absorber mount shattered, or the accelerator pedal stuck. There may have been a spot of grease on the highway, or a pothole, or perhaps it was raining or windy

21

that day. And, finally, if the tree had not been right where it was, maybe the car would simply have bumped to a stop and the driver would have walked away.

Traffic safety experts know that automobile accidents are complicated occurrences, with a multitude of causes which may or may not be present in any given mishap. This is the reason traffic accidents are such a difficult problem.

The odd thing is that many people who would be easily convinced of the complexity of such a commonplace event as an automobile accident still want to assign simple causes to the riots in Negro ghettos. They're a Communist plot. Or riots are the result of coddling criminals — not cracking down hard enough in high crime areas. Or they happen because civil rights militants are stirring up the Negroes. Or Negroes are just criminal people, out for anything they can get.

These attitudes arise mostly out of ignorance. Even the reasons for this ignorance are complicated, but ignorance is not the subject here.

As with most oversimplifications, however, there is some truth in even the most apparently absurd reasons for the explosions in ghetto areas of several cities in the summer of 1967.

The Communist conspiracy theory is an example. There is little doubt that there are a few Communists running around trying to stir Negroes to revolution. But saying that is not the same thing as saying — as the John Birch Society says — that the riots, even the civil rights movement for that matter, are part of a Communist plot to take over the United States. Dick Gregory, the civil rights leader and comedian, says people who think this are so ignorant that they cannot believe Negroes could be legitimately angry on their own. And, as he has pointed out many times, there could not possibly be enough Communists in the United States to cover every street corner in every urban ghetto in the country every night of the week, waiting for an incident that might be the excuse to incite a riot.

The prestigious United States Advisory Commission on Civil Disorders, after completing its monumental study of the summer 1967 riots, concluded: "The urban disorders . . . were not caused by, nor were they the consequence of, any organized plan or 'conspiracy.' Specifically, the Commission has found no evidence that all or any of the disorders or the incidents that led to them were planned or directed by any organization or group, international, national or local."

No, riots cannot be dismissed simply as Communist exploitation of social problems. Riots are the result of a legacy of repression in the United States, of unfulfilled promises, of an American dream that never came true for nearly 11 percent of the population.

Negroes have been Americans longer than any distinguishable group except Indian-Americans. But they have not reached the degree of freedom and justice the country accords to the immigrant who arrived less than ten years ago. The Hungarian Freedom Fighters who rebelled against Russian domination there in 1956, then fled to the United States, already have been assimilated into the country. Yet some of them have had the nerve to become self-righteous about riots in Negro ghettos.

I am no more anti-Hungarian than I am anti-anything, yet it disgusted me when a Hungarian Freedom Fighter organization in Milwaukee felt constrained to express its indignation over a statement by Father Groppi comparing Milwaukee's rioters to Hungarian Freedom Fighters. Whether the comparison was valid is beside the point. The Hungarians came to the United States for freedom and found it, yet some of them rush to disassociate themselves from a group of Americans still struggling to obtain the same freedom they enjoy. Many white noncitizens of the United States reap more of the fruits of freedom than Afro-Americans, whose roots in this country go back 350 years. A sociologist once told me that white Americans were really responsible for Negro riots — and not only because their racism had suppressed the Negro's legitimate desire for a share of American democracy. He said that the trouble with white America was that it always had preached one thing and practiced another. We preached the concept of the great melting pot, of equal opportunity for all, of freedom for every citizen. If we had not told Negroes that they were part of the American dream, if we had told them right along that they had to be satisfied with second-class citizenship, perhaps there would be no rioting today.

The sociologist was speaking somewhat tongue-in-cheek. But what he said is true. Alexis de Tocqueville, the famed French historian, saw it as far back as the early nineteenth century, when he wrote: "The sufferings that are endured patiently, as being inevitable, become intolerable the moment that it appears that there might be an escape."

Americans have been preaching one thing and practicing something else. The United States Advisory Commission put it this way:

"What white Americans have never fully understood — but what the Negro can never forget — is that white society is deeply implicated in the ghetto. White institutions created it, white institutions maintain it, and white society condones it." And now, with the country blanketed by modern communications, the preaching, along with its unfulfilled promises, reaches everyone.

The modern communications media — radio, television, newspapers, books, and magazines — have to take at least part of the rap for the riots. The responsibility is incidental, indirect, and inadvertent, but nonetheless real. Television is particularly responsible.

The United States Census Bureau estimates that there are television sets in 94 out of every 100 homes in the country. Sets have become cheap and plentiful. Many models sell for less than $100. To a poor family, a TV set is an investment in entertainment — in some cases, it might be the only entertainment the family has. Even in southern cities, where unpainted shacks on concrete blocks line unpaved streets, television antennas can be seen sticking up from the rooftops.

As a result, the poor, Negro as well as white, have an open door to the world. They see the news events of the day, as well as the advertising industry's distorted view of the Good Life in the United States, a view which simultaneously reflects and strengthens that of society in general.

There sits an urban ghetto dweller. His plumbing leaks or perhaps does not work at all, rotted electrical wiring presents an ever present fire hazard, floorboards creak and sometimes break, and the rats and cockroaches run boldly through the house. Yet he watches the "be young and fair and debonair" commercials on television, the Beautiful People, suntanned and carefree, who populate a world of new homes, fine furniture, green lawns, two cars in the garage, vacations in the country — in short, a world he has no hope of living in.

That ghetto dweller is an individual human being, worth more in and of himself than all the accouterments that tantalize him on the television screen. He has likes and dislikes, aversions and desires, feelings and insensitivities that are natural to any person. And he wants a piece of the action. He wants the Good Life as much as any white suburbanite.

But he is one of society's have-nots, unemployed or underemployed. It matters little if he is black or white — there are many white have-nots, too. But it is worse for the black man because he has less chance of breaking out of the ghetto and being assimilated into the mainstream of society. To most of the white majority, he is a Negro first and an individual second.

Put this man out on the street on a summer night. There is an incident — a riot breaks out. Store windows are smashed and crowds gather, as they did in Detroit and other cities. The man might not have participated up to this point, except as a spectator. But there in front of him is a broken display window. Radios, television sets, cameras, other appliances are there for the taking. So he takes something. There is anonymity in the crowd and apparently little likelihood of getting caught. The situation is analogous to a white suburbanite speeding on a freeway because he doesn't think he will be caught. The ghetto dweller thinks the same way. What has he got to lose?

Maybe his life — shot down as a looter. But he doesn't think about that, just as the freeway speeder doesn't think that he will be involved in a traffic accident. It matters not whether he is black or white — whites looted as readily as blacks in the Detroit riot. In Milwaukee, the situation was different, but only because the riot was confined to a neighborhood that was almost all Negro and because police held looting to a minimum by guarding stores and other business places.

There is another, perhaps minor, aspect of the riots that can be tied to the communications media. Ever since Watts — some have called Watts the prototype riot — the urban riots have been covered extensively by television, radio, newspapers, and magazines, with the result that almost everyone in the United States knows exactly how to go about conducting a riot. You start with an incident, usually involving the police. Then you break windows, follow that up with fire bombs and looting, and then, if you are of a mind, you get a gun and start sniping to harass police and firemen. The pattern has been repeated in every city.

Race tension certainly is another factor in riots. Resentment against "Mr. Charlie" is high among some Negroes, particularly against the white man in the blue uniform. The US Advisory Commission, in its "Profile of a Rioter," concluded that the typical rioter was extremely hostile to whites. However, the commission added that "his hostility is more apt to be a product of social and economic class than of race; he is almost equally hostile toward middle-class Negroes."

Some Negroes, of course, are plainly prejudiced against whites. Oddly enough, this fact seems to shock a lot of white people. This is amusing reverse-English thinking. It never seems to shock whites that their white co-workers and friends are prejudiced against Negroes. Yet they express horror and indignation when they hear black militants openly shouting anti-white epithets.

But it has been my experience that Negroes are less prejudiced and a great deal more sensible about race than whites. While a black man may vilify "whitey" as much as some whites degrade Negroes, it usually has nothing to do with his relationships on a man-to-man basis. The prejudice among Negroes appears to be more suspicion than bigotry. All a white person has to do, in most cases, is show that he is honest and a man of goodwill. The prejudice against him, as a whitey, melts away. Perhaps no black leader ever was as antiwhite as the late Malcolm X. Yet Malcolm himself discovered that a man's worth depended on his attitude rather than his skin color. In a speech after his return from a Muslim pilgrimage to Mecca in 1964, Malcolm said:

My pilgrimage broadened my scope. It blessed me with a new insight. In two weeks in the Holy Land, I saw what I never had seen in thirty-nine years in America. I saw all *races,* all *colors,* — blue-eyed blonds to black-skinned Africans — in *true* brotherhood! In unity! Living as one! Worshiping as one! No segregationists — no liberals; they would not have known how to interpret the meaning of those words.

In the past, yes, I have made sweeping indictments of *all* white people. I never will be guilty of that again — as I know now that some white people *are* truly sincere, that some truly are capable of being brotherly toward a black man. The true Islam has shown me that a blanket indictment of all white people is as wrong as when whites make blanket indictments against blacks.

Yes, I have been convinced that *some* American Whites do want to help cure the rampant racism which is on the path to *destroying* this country!

It was in the Holy World that my attitude was changed, by what I experienced there, and by what I witnessed there, in terms of brotherhood — not just brotherhood toward me, but brotherhood between all men, of all nationalities and complexions, who were there. And now that I am back in America, my attitude here concerning white people has to be governed by what my black brothers and I experience here, and what we witness here — in terms of brotherhood. The *problem* here in America is that we meet such a small minority of individual so-called "good," or "brotherly" white people. Here in the United States, notwithstanding those few "good" white people, it is the *collective* 150 million white people whom the *collective* 22 million black people have to deal with!

Why, here in America, the seeds of racism are so deeply rooted in the white people collectively, their belief that they are "superior" in some way is so deeply rooted, that these things are in the national white sub-consciousness. Many whites are even actually unaware of their own racism, until they face some test, and then their racism emerges in one form or another.

Malcolm had it pegged. In 1968, the President's Advisory Commission on Civil Disorders concluded: "White racism is essentially responsible for the explosive mixture which has been accumulating in our cities since the end of World War II."

Whites often point to the "progress" made by Negroes in the past few years, particularly with the passage of the Civil Rights Act of 1964 and the Voting Rights Act of 1965. The trouble with such progress is that it has made little difference to the man in the ghetto of the big northern city. He may still be on relief because he cannot find a job, paying high rent for an overcrowded, dilapidated apartment because no one will rent to him in a better neighborhood. The big federal laws have not helped him.

Indeed, they may have deepened the wounds. The president's commission concluded: "Frustrated hopes are the residue of the unfulfilled expectations aroused by the great judicial and legislative victories of the Civil Rights Movement and the dramatic struggle for equal rights in the South."

The ghetto dweller is disenchanted over the failure of these victories to materially affect his everyday existence. He sees, too, how any city that has been hit by a riot begins scrambling to do something about his problems and those of his neighbors. Perhaps he begins to feel that violence is the only way to shake up the power structure enough to get it working on programs that will benefit him and his family directly. "The frustrations of powerlessness," said the commission, "have led some Negroes to the conviction that there is no effective alternative to violence as a means of achieving redress of grievances, and of 'moving the system.' "

Most Negroes are as frightened by a riot as any white, and the vast majority of them have not and never would participate in one. But many Negroes, even those among the rich and middle class, understand why some of their brothers riot. "There's a bitterness against a white face," says Mrs. Ardie Halyard, a long-time Milwaukee resident and a leading member of Milwaukee's Negro community. "Negroes can understand why they have been bitter and angry, and disillusioned with the whole setup." Mrs. Halyard and her late husband, Wilbur, founded a savings and loan association in Milwaukee. A Milwaukee street is named after Mr. Halyard.

Negroes can understand because many of them have experienced, to at least some degree, the frustrations that lead to rioting — the "pervasive discrimination and segregation in employment, education and housing, which have resulted in the continuing exclusion of great numbers of Negroes from the benefits of economic progress" — in the words of the president's commission.

This, too, is why you can find few Negroes who would condemn outright the black nationalist militants. The antiwhite nationalists appear to be few in numbers, perhaps so few as to be nearly nonexistent in cities like Milwaukee. It also would seem doubtful that any of them could command a large following, in the sense of others taking up arms and following them into a revolutionary battle in the streets.

Yet there is a great deal of what might be called "soul brother" support for a man like Stokely Carmichael. It is a sort of "moral support," in the sense of people saying, "He's telling it like it is" — telling the truth.

What many of the black power militants say, in essence, is that black people in America have gotten nowhere with nonviolent demonstrations in appealing to the white man's sense of morality. And Negroes cannot negotiate to gain equality, they say, because they have no chips to bring to the bargaining table. According to this line of argument, the only thing black people can provide as an incentive to whites is a threat — "either give us our rightful place in society or we will destroy it."

The militants can offer convincing evidence to back up these arguments. They can point out that riots have prompted positive results for Negro ghettos. In the six months following the Detroit riot, for example, the New Detroit Committee — composed of leading business and civic leaders, along with militant blacks — opened up 50,000 new jobs. More than half of them went to Negroes.

Whitney M. Young, Jr., executive director of the National Urban League, argues against the idea that riots produce results. He says that a riot may get 3,000 jobs for Negroes, but at the same time might scuttle a chance for congressional action that would, in the long run, produce 300,000 jobs. Yet even Young understands why black people riot. And he says the main reason he is against riots is because he does not think Negroes can win that way. Young's approach is to put the pressure on white business and industrial leaders, and he has been successful at it.

Whether the more extreme black militants actually have started riots in some of the big cities is doubtful. Their role would seem to fit in more with the riot ingredient cited by the Civil Disorders Commission. This ingredient is the "climate that tends toward approval and encouragement of violence as a form of protest." The climate, the commission said, "has been created by white terrorism directed against nonviolent protest; by the open defiance of law and federal authority by state and local officials resisting desegregation; and by some protest groups engaging in civil disobedience who turn their backs on nonviolence, go beyond the constitutionally protected rights of petition and free assembly, and resort to violence to attempt to compel alteration of laws and policies with which they disagree."

The hard core criminal element in riots cannot be ignored. Some habitual criminals no doubt have taken advantage of riot situations to line their own pockets. Yet the majority of those arrested in riots have been people with no police records or records for only minor offenses. In the Watts riot of 1965, for example, a total of 3,371 persons were arrested. Of those, 867 had no previous police record at all, another 965 had been arrested previously but had not been convicted. (Many slum dwellers can testify how easy it is to get arrested in a ghetto area.) Only 363 had served prison terms prior to being arrested during the riot. The remainder had been convicted previously of a variety of major and minor offenses, most of which resulted in sentences of less that 90 days.

Riots have perhaps as many causes as there are people involved. No man can look into another man's brain to find out why he did something; perhaps the individual himself has little, if any, idea of what motivated him to do what he did. Even the riot commission's "profile of a rioter" offers only a general clue to the individual involved. It describes the typical rioter as between 15 and 24 years old, a life-long resident of the city in which the riot took place, better educated — though not a high school graduate — than the average inner city Negro, working in a menial job, proud of being black, hostile to whites, better informed about politics than the nonriot Negro, and extremely distrustful of political leaders.

The riot factors sketched here are possibilities, not certainties. Any or all of them, or none of them, could have been reasons why particular individuals participated in riots. Their main value is to show that there are no simple answers, that anyone who fancies himself expert enough to pinpoint a single cause for the conflagrations is deluded or an outright liar.

It cannot be emphasized too strongly that riots are people — individual people, each with his or her particular traits and problems. In a world of automation and computers, we tend to forget that each of those 10 traffic fatalities, 76 dead in an airplane crash, or 43 in a riot, was an individual. Yet, incongruously, we sometimes place high value on the life of one person. We have spent millions of dollars searching for the one last survivor of a shipwreck, heedless of the material costs.

In a natural disaster — flood, tornado, or snowstorm — an entire city can and does mobilize to help the small percentage of people affected. Government works hand in hand with the private sector with but one goal in mind — to relieve the suffering of the people.

It is a scandal that similar steps have not been taken to relieve the suffering in the black ghettos of our big cities.

IV

GEMÜTLICHKEIT AND STEREOTYPES

Cities, as well as people, are stereotyped. Chicago is the Windy City, Detroit the Motor City, and Milwaukee is Beertown USA — despite the fact that brewing is only a minor industry in Milwaukee. With cities, most of the stereotypes — especially those that show them in a favorable light — are carefully nurtured to instill community pride in the people who live there and to attract other people to move there. The bad images are downplayed; the good ones are advertised.

So it has been with Milwaukee. No brochure advertised that the city had slums, poor people, or a definite strain of bigotry. Milwaukee was the city of beer and good times, a clean city, a place to raise a family, the city of gemütlichkeit — that untranslatable German word that means well-being and contentment.

But by the end of 1967 it had another stereotype tacked on. It was a place where people were afraid to walk the streets at night. Never mind that the fears were, for the most part, founded on distorted information; that it was no less safe to walk the streets at the end of 1967 than it had been at the beginning of the year. Outsiders, and even many people who lived there, believed that it was not safe, and that was what counted, that was what worried the businessmen and the other people who are paid to worry about a city's economy. It was not unlike the belief about police brutality that existed in the city's Negro area. The belief, not the fact, was the important thing.

Milwaukee's image was badly tarnished, first by a riot in its

31

Negro ghetto, and then, later, by a riot on the south side in which whites chanted, "We want slaves!" and attacked an integrated group marching to demonstrate their desire for an open housing law. The image was worse outside Milwaukee because of national press coverage that maximized the violence.

⸙But even in the city, some of the fear approached the ridiculous. In an inner core business place months after the riot and the open housing demonstrations, a white woman showed me a revolver she kept handy. That did not surprise me, but then she told me that she kept another pistol hidden in a roaster at home in case Negroes should bother her. I asked where she lived. Her home, she said, was in a suburban subdivision out near the Milwaukee-Waukesha county line — more than ten miles from the inner core.

The fear ate away at Milwaukee's proud stature as one of the nation's most prosperous urban centers. Milwaukee, the nation's eleventh largest city, could boast of many things in 1967. Although it produced more beer than any city in the country, the major industries actually were in the production of durable goods — construction and road building machinery; gasoline, gas turbine, and diesel engines; electrical machinery and controls, machine tools; agricultural equipment, iron and steel castings, automotive equipment, and precision instruments and measuring devices.

Milwaukee was the hub of a three county metropolitan area of nearly 1.4 million people. It had a long standing reputation for corruption-free government, a police department nationally recognized as one of the best in the nation in terms of its ability to catch criminals and keep the crime rate down, a park system operated by Milwaukee county that was second to none in the nation, an international port on Lake Michigan, a good school system for most of its people, a vocational school system hailed as one of the best in the world, and low unemployment.

But in a few short months in the last half of 1967, the image was shattered. It will take years for the city to re-establish its stereotype as a pleasant, comfortable city with few problems. Mayor Maier blamed it on the press coverage of Milwaukee's riot and open housing demonstrations — particularly the national press coverage. There was validity in the criticism, but it was an oversimplification.

The fear that crippled Milwaukee had been a long time coming, but in some ways it had been inevitable. Wisconsin had Negroes as far back as 1746. Nearly 100 years later, on September 18, 1835, a

Negro voted in the town of Milwaukee's first election. His name was Joe Oliver and he was a cook for Solomon Juneau, one of the city's founding fathers.

In some ways Milwaukee and Wisconsin were more forward looking on race relations in the nineteenth century than they were in the twentieth century. The Wisconsin constitution, ratified in 1848 — more than a decade before the Civil War — prohibited slavery. It also contained a provision authorizing the state legislature to hold a referendum on the question of Negro suffrage.

The referendum was conducted in 1849. A majority of those who went to the polls favored voting rights for Negroes. However, the referendum was invalidated by a technicality. There was a question of whether the constitutional provision demanded a majority of votes on the referendum question itself or a majority of the votes cast in the entire election. The question was put to referendums again in 1857 and 1865, but this time it was voted down.

In the 1865 election, a Negro in Milwaukee tried to vote but was refused. He took the matter to court. The following year the Wisconsin supreme court ruled that the 1849 referendum had been valid all along and that Negroes had had the right to vote. The suffrage question was settled — never again to be raised.

Before the turn of the century, as the result of a public clamor in Milwaukee, the state passed a law guaranteeing everyone access to public accommodations regardless of race, creed, national origin, or ancestry. The clamor came about after an usher refused to allow a Negro to sit in a seat for which he had bought a ticket in the old Bijou Opera House. A prominent Episcopal clergyman spearheaded the drive, accusing the theater of "contemptible barbarism." In 1889, as a result of the incident, Milwaukee's Negroes held a civil rights convention and, according to one historian, drafted the public accommodations law.

The bill listed inns, restaurants, saloons, barbershops, theaters, land and water conveyances, and "all other places of public accommodation or amusement." It said these places should be open to all persons and also specified that no one could be required to pay more than a regular rate for services.

The bill was introduced into the predominantly Democratic legislature in 1891. At that time, there were only 2,444 Negroes out of a total population of 1,680,000 in the state. The Milwaukee Negro Population was 449, or .22 percent of the total of 204,468.

The law was defeated, and lay dormant until after the Republicans came to power in 1894. Then it was introduced simultaneously in both houses of the legislature and, with little discussion, passed. It provided a maximum penalty for violation of a $100 fine and six months in jail. The law remains on the books today with only minor variations. In 1965, Wisconsin's limited open housing law became an amendment to the 1895 law.

By the turn of the century, Negroes still comprised only a fraction of one percent of the total city population. It was not until World War I and the need it generated for increased numbers of workers that Negroes began coming to the city in any significant numbers. The Negro population in the city jumped more than 125 percent between 1910 and 1920, but it still made up only one-half of one percent of the total.

Milwaukee did not get the large numbers of migrating Negroes that other cities did, partly because many southern Negroes who came north stopped at Chicago. Those Negroes who did find their way to Milwaukee found a city that was predominantly German and as totally segregated as any southern city. Restrictive covenants in deeds, combined with a widespread "understanding," kept Negroes in a small area of a few square blocks just north of the downtown area.

By 1930, there were 7,501 Negroes in Milwaukee — a jump of more than 236 percent over the 2,229 in 1920 — and Milwaukee's Negro neighborhood had expanded. It was four blocks long and three blocks wide. The population density there was twice that of the average for the city. Milwaukee's Socialist mayor, Daniel W. Hoan, appointed a committee to study Negro housing in the city. The committee reported back that building spacing, heating, and sanitary facilities in the area were below average.

The city then started a program to ultimately demolish all below standard buildings in the city. As one historian put it in 1967: "No target date was set for this objective, which may have been just as well. There have been scores of other committee reports since then, along with considerable razing of buildings and some construction, but the ultimate day has not arrived."

By the end of the depression years, studies showed that more than half of the homes in Milwaukee that were unfit for human habitation were occupied by Negroes.

The black population in the city increased only slightly before the onset of World War II — to 8,821. This was still only 1.5 percent of the total population at that time of 587,472, not enough for the majority of Milwaukee's burghers to be concerned about. This lack of concern for a minority suffering discrimination was not, of course, confined to Milwaukee.

Milwaukee and the rest of the country still had a chance at this point to correct the inadequacies. The riots of 1967 could have been prevented 25 years ago. It was not for lack of information that these steps were not taken. Swedish sociologist Gunnar Myrdal had provided the insights and the necessary information in his classic study, *An American Dilemma.*

Another war and the shortage of manpower again brought increased numbers of Negroes to Milwaukee. The war also had the side effect of fostering some desegregation. Because of the war effort and the lack of workers to man the industries, many plants that heretofore had been totally segregated began to hire Negroes. However, the cancellation of military contracts at the end of the war put 1,500 Negroes out of work.

But Negroes still could not buy homes or rent outside of the inner core area. Negro servicemen — Milwaukee contributed about 1,000 — had to go to a Negro USO. There were no Negro high school teachers in the city. The Negro was still the last hired and the first fired. By 1950, there were 21,772 Negroes living in the city — more than 3 percent of the total population.

However, this still was not enough to arouse any particular concern among Milwaukeeans. Negroes then, as they still do, moved where they could find housing — usually in the city's inner core. The core then was an island in the city, an area not more than a mile square. White Milwaukee mostly ignored its black minority.

In the next ten years, the Negro population leaped nearly 187 percent, to 62,458, or more than 8.4 percent of the total population. And, as they had all along, Negroes moved into the inner core because, for the most part, they were denied housing in white neighborhoods. The inner core itself, however, expanded as the population increased. Whites fled from the fringes of the Negro neighborhoods and the boundaries of the inner core bulged outward to the west and north. 1960 census takers found most of Milwaukee's Negroes living in an area of about 5.3 square miles.

Most of the city's Negroes still lived in that area, but by the end of 1967 the black population had climbed to about 90,000, or about

12 percent of the total number of 774,000 residents. That 12 percent lived in only 5.5 percent of the total land area in the city, making Milwaukee one of the most segregated cities in the country. Except for a few families, the Negro neighborhood was almost as well-defined as it had been in the thirties.

Late in 1967, the district director of the Federal Housing Administration redefined the area from 5.3 to about 7.9 square miles. An FHA study showed that only about 320 Negro families lived outside the area, most of them on the northwest side of the city, which was the closest thing Milwaukee had to what might be called an integrated neighborhood.

There were only 66 Negro families in 25 suburban cities and villages that ring the city. Eight of those cities had no Negroes at all. In 1965, in a similar survey I did for a story for *The Milwaukee Journal,* I found only 60 Negro families in 19 of 30 suburban communities.

To a casual observer, in the summer of 1967, the heart of Milwaukee's inner core did not appear to fit the usual stereotype of a slum neighborhood. There were no dilapidated row houses on bare streets as in Philadelphia, no tenements as in New York city. Most of the housing consisted of single family homes and duplexes, along with some apartment buildings. The neighborhoods were similar, in some ways, to those in Detroit that were hit by rioting that same summer. Milwaukee's inner core homes were on wide, tree lined streets, not unlike many poorer white neighborhoods in the city.

To anyone who was simply passing through, the area did not look as slummy as those in some other cities. But a closer look revealed the litter, broken glass, and abandoned automobiles that characterize the typical ghetto area. People lived in rundown homes with rats and roaches, plumbing that did not work, heating systems that conked out on cold days, broken windows that went unrepaired — all typical of slum housing anywhere.

The problems in the summer of 1967 were particularly gross in an area of the west side of the inner core that was scheduled for demolition in an urban renewal project. This area, designated Kilbourntown 3, was the most neglected in the city. Owners made little or no repairs on homes that were to be torn down anyway. Many houses stood vacant, their windows broken and insides gutted by vandals. Fires — some believed started by the owners themselves — were common.

The plight of the people living under these conditions was complicated by the fact that Milwaukee's urban renewal program had produced almost nothing in terms of help for low income families. On paper, the city's urban renewal projects looked impressive — 22 projects, many of them aimed at clearing slums or rehabilitating neighborhoods in the inner core. But most of the projects still were in the planning stages.

One that was completed produced nearly 600 new apartments, but the trouble here was the trouble that most other cities with similar projects faced — the people the project was designed to help could not afford the rents. About the only projects that provided help to residents of the inner core were public housing. And these perpetuated the segregation in the city because south side Milwaukee aldermen for years steadfastly refused to permit any public housing on the all-white south side, thereby also blocking this sort of assistance for the white elderly and the white poor.

Schools also were a sore point with Milwaukee's inner core residents. The city school board had adamantly refused for several years to take any positive action toward reducing de facto segregation, with the result that as of summer, 1967, most of the schools in Milwaukee's inner core area remained predominantly Negro.

The school board had adhered to a policy of "compensatory education" — extra help for the disadvantaged — for the inner core schools. Yet even those programs were sharply criticized by researchers who conducted a comprehensive study of the entire Milwaukee public school system. Many school officials, the study said, had little understanding of the Negro child's problems.

As in other cities, employment also was a serious problem. Although there were no specific statistics, estimates of Negro unemployment in the city put the rate at two to three times that of the white population. Many businesses and industries in the metropolitan area had dropped racial barriers to employment. Their complaint was that qualified Negroes could not be found. The problem was an old and familiar one. Ghetto existence, poor education, and discrimination had put many Negroes in the position of being able to qualify for only the meanest of jobs — jobs that themselves were rapidly disappearing.

The Milwaukee ghetto also was an area of high crime — from that standpoint, the most undesirable place in the city to live. Police department statistics showed that Negroes were arrested in connection with 45 percent of the major crimes committed in the city.

It can be argued, with some validity, that the statistics overemphasize the situation, partly because the Negro neighborhoods were policed more closely than white neighborhoods. One of the reasons for this is that ghetto areas generally offered a great deal more anonymity for the criminal and potential criminal. The areas attracted the criminal element. Because these areas were more closely policed, a person who committed a crime was more likely to be arrested. And because it was an area of high crime, anyone was more likely to be arrested as a suspect.

Another factor in the high crime rate in the inner core was the age of the Negro population. Police singled out juvenile crime as one of their major problems, and a 1963 study showed that 43 percent of Milwaukee's Negro population was under 15 years of age while the figure was only 28 percent for the white majority. More than half of Milwaukee's Negroes were under 25 years of age.

All of these issues — education, employment, housing, crime, and police — had been touched on by civil rights militants in Milwaukee. The civil rights movement in the city developed later than it did in many other cities around the country. It was not until the historic march on Washington in 1963 that Milwaukee experienced extensive civil rights demonstrations. There had been social action and civil rights organizations such as the Milwaukee Urban League and the local branch of the NAACP. But neither had made many headlines.

The Milwaukee civil rights movement had four distinct periods involving three separate militant organizations — the Congress of Racial Equality, the Milwaukee United School Integration Committee and the Milwaukee NAACP Youth Council. There were four main issues: A controversial appointment of a member of a commission set up to solve the city's racial and poverty problems, de facto segregation in the city's public schools, the membership of public officials in a segregated private club, and open housing.

The civil rights organizations won minor victories in these campaigns, but for the most part their protests went unheeded. No one can say for certain, but it may be that if the city had listened more closely to what they were saying, there would have been no riot in the summer of 1967.

V

CORE COMES OUT OF THE CORE

Fred E. Lins was one of many Milwaukeeans in 1963 who showed little comprehension of the problems of the city's black citizens and of the civil rights militancy that was beginning to stir in the ghettos of many northern cities.

At the time Lins was appointed to the city's new Community Social Development Commission, civil rights still was primarily a southern movement, battling for legal victories against segregation in schools and public facilities, and seeking to remove discriminatory barriers against Negroes who might have wanted to exercise their constitutional right to vote.

It was a time when northerners could beat their breasts and bewail the terrible conditions under which Negroes lived in the deep south, when they congratulated themselves that such conditions did not exist in the north. It was a time of Afghanistanism, when newspaper editorial writers, public officials, and ordinary citizens expressed righteous indignation over the plight of the black man in the southern United States, while ignoring the worse plight of many Negroes right in their own back yards.

It was not long before they were rudely awakened. In July of 1963 in Milwaukee, a small group of Negroes and whites formed a new chapter of the militant Congress of Racial Equality, a nonviolent, integrated organization that had conducted sit-ins and freedom rides in the south to protest segregated public accommodations and transportation.

In less than a week, the new core chapter had its first civil rights issue — Fred Lins, president and treasurer of a sausage manufacturing company in the inner core.

The Community Social Development Commission had first been proposed back in May of 1962 by Mayor Maier. Its stated purpose was to coordinate community action on social problems of juvenile delinquency, the aged, and Negroes in the city's inner core. The commission was made up of representatives of the city, Milwaukee County, the Milwaukee School Board, the Milwaukee Vocational School, and the United Fund. Lins was appointed as one of the county representatives.

It was not long before he became the most widely known member of the commission. Like so many people, then and now, Lins sought simple answers to the complex problems with which he was supposed to deal as a member of the commission. He said that some way had to be found to keep the ignorant poor from migrating to Milwaukee. New arrivals to the city, he said, were taking advantage of people who already lived there.

Near the end of the newspaper story relating Lins's "solution" were other comments that led to Milwaukee's first civil rights sit-ins. Lins was quoted as saying, "The Negroes look so much alike that you can't identify the ones that committed the crime." He also was quoted as saying that, among Negroes, "An awful mess of them have an IQ of nothing."

Later, Lins contended that he had been quoted out of context, although he did concede that some of the things he had said were "unfortunate and ill-advised." He insisted that he was not prejudiced and could serve impartially on the new commission. In his own mind, Lins no doubt was convinced that he was not prejudiced. And, he no doubt reflected the thinking of the majority of white Milwaukee. But his statements did indicate that he was the victim of stereotyped ideas about Negroes and, as a result, lacked the basic understanding needed to work on the problems that would come before the new commission.

In the view of the members of the new CORE chapter, Lins's statements showed bigotry. The chapter wasted little time. Five days after the story quoting Lins appeared, and less than two weeks after it was organized, CORE picketed Lins's sausage company.

The historic March on Washington intervened. Many Milwaukee

CORE members traveled to the nation's capital by bus to be among the more than 200,000 persons who marched on the Lincoln Memorial to dramatize the grievances of the country's Negroes. But enough CORE members remained so that Milwaukee's first major civil rights demonstration could coincide with the Washington march. On August 28, 1963, while Negroes and whites massed at the monument to the Great Emancipator, nine members of the Milwaukee CORE chapter conducted Milwaukee's first sit-in demonstration in the county courthouse. The purpose was to demand that the county board chairman, Eugene F. Grobschmidt, fire Lins from his post on the Social Development Commission.

Grobschmidt's reaction was at least partly responsible for prompting the sit-in. His reply, when the CORE chapter demanded Lins's ouster, was "I'm not going to ask him to resign because of his personal beliefs." The notion that such personal beliefs might not be in keeping with the purposes of the new commission apparently was not a consideration.

CORE's demonstrations against the Lins appointment continued for more than three weeks. There were sit-ins at the courthouse, picketing, and even a "phone-in," when members of the chapter tied up the courthouse switchboard with more than 600 calls demanding that Lins be removed from the commission.

The protest also found its way into Mayor Maier's office. CORE asked the mayor to repudiate Lins. When he refused, CORE members sat in at his office. About two dozen persons in all were arrested during the three weeks of demonstrations. On September 21, John H. Givens, Jr., the young Negro chairman of the CORE chapter, called off the picketing and other demonstrations, saying that the issue had been sufficiently dramatized. He announced that CORE would concentrate its efforts on employment discrimination and slum landlords.

Givens was a handsome, personable young man who had tasted equality. As a GI in France in 1961, he developed so strong a friendship with the residents of a small town in Normandy called Pont L'Eveque that they petitioned President John F. Kennedy to let Givens stay when he was ordered back to the United States. The petition got nowhere, but the villagers of Pont L'Eveque had left their imprint on Givens. "Take this thing about equality," he said when he returned to Milwaukee. "Never has an individual been more different than me from these people, yet I was just like one of the family. If people who are different in race would meet the challenge squarely, this thing can work." Milwaukee was not meeting the challenge, and Givens wound up as a leader in the civil rights movement.

The reaction in Milwaukee to its first major civil rights demonstration was not unlike the city's reaction to more recent civil rights demonstrations. Instead of focusing on the issue at hand, the demonstrators themselves became the issue to most Milwaukeeans. A state senator who represented the south side typified the feeling. He said he planned to introduce legislation to ban picketing or demonstrations inside public or private buildings. Demonstrations, he said, belonged on the sidewalk.

To the majority of Milwaukeeans, a prejudicial viewpoint on a commission designed to deal, in part, with the problems of Negroes was excusable. The fact that a group of citizens protested was not. And the state senator would try to pass a law to restrict the constitutional rights of every citizen to prevent a few from exercising those rights.

The CORE demonstrations produced little in the way of results for anyone concerned, beyond the fact that some of the protesters wound up in jail. Lins finally resigned from the Social Development Commission the following December. But he cited poor health as the reason.

The demonstrations did show, however, that Milwaukee was not fated to escape criticism for its deficiencies. Not that many Milwaukeeans even considered that the city had anything wrong with it; indeed, many people to this day cannot understand why anyone would want to conduct a civil rights demonstration in the city. But this sort of community myopia was and is not confined to Milwaukee.

The Social Development Commission's troubles were not over, although its membership never again became the target of a civil rights demonstration. In August of 1964, the commission was designated as the official agency in Milwaukee to administer money from the Economic Opportunity Act — the federal war on poverty. During more than two years after that, the commission tangled itself in organizational problems and haggled over the federal government's requirement that the poor participate in antipoverty planning. It was not until early in 1967 that the poor finally were given a voice on the commission, which by then had been renamed the Community Relations-Social Development Commission in Milwaukee County.

The difficulty with the commission was the same difficulty that has plagued commissions and committees in Milwaukee and elsewhere. This is the notion that you can somehow solve problems by forming a committee of solid citizens of reasonably good will used to doing things in a traditional manner. It has not worked, either in Milwaukee or anywhere else, because such committees and commissions usually reflect an "I know what's good for you so you do it my way or not at all" attitude. Solving modern problems of poverty and civil rights takes expertise, imagination, foresight, and, above all, a deep understanding of the problems and people, along with involvement of the people themselves. It does not need people who simply like to serve on committees or commissions, or statements like participation of the poor being "an obvious threat to local government control."

Out of sight of the public eye in that summer of 1963, Milwaukee's power structure was beginning to stir. It was not precisely a reaction to the CORE demonstrations; rather it was a reaction to the civil rights militancy that was beginning to make itself felt in northern cities. At almost the same time, Milwaukee's Negro leadership sensed the growing urgency.

The movement of the white power structure started with a private meeting — at the mayor's request — between Mayor Maier and Irwin Maier, president of the Journal Company and publisher of *The Milwaukee Journal* and the *Milwaukee Sentinel*. The two men, who are not related, discussed civil rights and the possible effects of the new militancy on Milwaukee. Mayor Maier wanted to know if there was a possibility of establishing a committee of business and professional leaders because, he said, civic rather than political leadership would be the most effective.

Publisher Maier, a man with a strong sense of personal community involvement, already had established himself as one of the most powerful movers in Milwaukee. He mentioned his conversation with the mayor to about half a dozen of his business associates and personal friends, all of whom also were civic leaders in the community.

Meanwhile, a group of Negro community leaders — educators, businessmen, clergymen, attorneys, doctors, and other professionals — had formed a group of their own called the Committee on a Statement of Concern. These 34 men had become increasingly concerned over problems in Milwaukee's Negro community and what they considered to be a lack of leadership by the mayor.

The community leaders — they were not civil rights leaders in the usual meaning of the term — developed a position paper to outline the issues as they saw them. They bought advertising space and published the "statement of concern" in the city's two newspapers on July 25. The statement covered the issues of jobs, education, housing, and lack of participation by Negroes in the Milwaukee decision making process. It was critical of the mayor and was shot through with a sense of urgency, even quoting President John F. Kennedy's prediction that those who failed to act on these problems were inviting violence.

The statement said:

We, the undersigned citizens, interested in establishing the kind of community where every individual may develop his full potential, are gravely concerned with the apparent negative reaction of official Milwaukee to the present rightful demands of this country's Negro population. The fact that these demands are in keeping with democratic principles is too elementary and fundamental for extended argument. In the present world-wide struggle for individual freedom, America cannot afford to waver in its commitment to democratic ideals lest the very foundations of freedom are endangered.

President John F. Kennedy, in his recent nation-wide address on civil rights, challenged all Americans to totally commit themselves to the realization of equal opportunity for all, regardless of race, religion, or national origin. The president thus set the moral tone for dealing with this crucial question, and committed himself and his administration to achieving this goal, the legal basis of which no longer can be doubted. Mr. Kennedy asked state and local leaders to fulfill their responsibilities in reaching a peaceful and immediate solution to this problem.

In view of these developments, it is disappointing that the mayor of our city, by his words and actions, has beclouded the hopes and aspirations of Milwaukee Negroes and the entire city of Milwaukee in achieving the goals so ably outlined by the president. Of course, this lack of concern with racial problems has been all too sadly apparent long before now.

Milwaukee has racial problems of a most serious nature. Attention must be given to these immediately if Milwaukee is to enjoy an orderly adjustment to social changes which are inevitable.

Fair housing policies are desperately needed in the city of Milwaukee. It is not enough to say that this is a problem of statewide concern — it is a problem which must be dealt with at both state and local levels. Legalisms and jurisdictional issues must give way to the realization of legislation designed to aid in the achievement of equal opportunity for good housing.

Employment opportunities for Negroes, both in the skilled and unskilled categories, are grossly inadequate. Unions have failed to provide adequate opportunities for apprenticeship training, and industry has not generally accepted Negroes in "on the job" training programs. Equal opportunity for decent jobs can instill human dignity and responsibility. Segregated neighborhoods in Milwaukee have resulted in de facto segregation of schools and recreational facilities. These need immediate attention.

In addition, we note the meager involvement and participation of Negroes in the operations of city government. Presently, too few Negroes serve on appointed policy making boards and commissions. Five Negroes are members of the Milwaukee Commission on Community Relations, which is only advisory and not policy making. We are keenly aware that political considerations are inevitably involved in the selection of such appointees. However, leadership in a democracy must consider incentive or motivational implications for involving, in a substantial way, the Negro segment of the community in running the affairs of the community. This is a must for self-government and an important consideration for the maintenance of a stable democratic society.

These problems are so closely interrelated that they must be attacked on all fronts in order to make meaningful achievements in any one area. These problems must be faced; they will not solve themselves. These problems must be dealt with in a constructive and progressive manner.

In this effort, the leadership of the mayor's office, despite its legal limitations, is imperative and essential. Could not the mayor, for example, following the leadership of President Kennedy, begin to use all the powers at his command — legal, persuasive, ceremonial and otherwise — to foster the kind of communication and co-operation between white and Negro leaders in these various areas? Could he not see that city hall policies, by his own example, influence that which community leaders do? Could not the mayor and common council provide moral leadership in the present crisis?

It is praiseworthy that the press (e.g., several editorials have appeared in *The Milwaukee Journal* and the *Milwaukee Star*), an important public opinion shaper with corresponding important responsibilities, has expressed its concern that city hall should assert more leadership in facing racial problems. As praiseworthy as this is, however, only the mayor has the overall vantage point, power and prestige to rally the kind of forces necessary, including the press, to cope with these problems.

The present mayor is in a position to make enduring the positive contributions in race relations. Whether he takes immediate action now can have an impact on all Milwaukee for many years to come, or he can remain complacent and allow the racial situation to worsen as it has in other communities.

As President Kennedy stated in his nation-wide address on civil rights, "Those who do nothing are inviting shame as well as violence. Those who act boldly are recognizing right as well as reality."

We call upon labor, business, the press, civic groups and churches to encourage the mayor to assume the responsibilities of leadership in this area of race relations. We call upon the common council to give leadership in this area also.

In a democracy, leaders sometimes have to deal with problems that might not be politically popular or expedient, but the solutions to which can bring about more enduring democratic foundations.

Four years and six days later, National Guard troops were speeding toward Milwaukee to back up policemen who were trying to quell the violence hinted at in the statement. And the fact of the situation was that the statement, with minor alterations, would have described the situation in Milwaukee as accurately in 1967 as it did in 1963.

The white civic leaders reacted by asking for a meeting with the Negro community leaders. Together, the two groups formed a new civic body to discuss minority group problems of employment, housing, and education. The new Committee of We — Milwaukeeans first met on September 25, 1963.

The committee was unusual in several respects. It had no formal organization; indeed, it did not have a separate existence of its own. The only time it existed as the Committee of We — Milwaukeeans was when the white civic leaders met in joint session with the executive directors of the Negro group. The white group, which in October organized itself as the Voluntary Industrial and Business Group, was separate from the Negro group, which maintained its own identity as the Committee of 34 or, as it sometimes was called, the Committee of Concern.

The Voluntary Industrial and Business Group was formed originally to work on the problem of minority group employment. Later, it widened its scope, and its name, and became the Voluntary Industrial, Labor and Business Group. Still later, the name became the Voluntary Associates.

We — Milwaukeeans was deliberately maintained as a loose-knit, voluntary organization with no power to make any of its decisions binding on anyone. Meetings were held secretly, so committee members could "let their hair down," and there were no news releases except by common consent. The thought was that committee members, particularly the white business and industry leaders, would shy away from any sort of formal organization.

Members of the Negro side of We — Milwaukeeans, for their part, were anxious to avoid any identification with the civil rights movement — an incongruous position in light of their original statement. Thomas M. Cheeks, the Negro co-chairman of We — Milwaukeeans, wrote: "I want to say that neither the Committee of 34 nor the executive committee of the Committee of 34 is to be considered a civil rights group or organization. We were not conceived with the idea of ever being a civil rights group, but rather a group that goes beyond the civil rights area — a group conceived with a positive program that hopefully will eliminate the need for civil rights legislation — eliminate the need for sit-ins, etc. — a group that by working toward these goals is attempting to make the American dream a reality."

The We — Milwaukeeans committee was, in a sense, hamstrung at the outset. It represented, among its white members at least, the economic power of the city. Yet it decided not to exert this power, either on its own members or on anyone else. Instead of being a pressure group, it was primarily a discussion group.

In defense of the committee, it should be said that many of its white members needed a great deal of convincing about the necessity for concerted action on the problems of Milwaukee's Negro minority. Some still were not totally convinced in 1967. It may be, too, that the committee never would have come into being if it had not adopted a strictly "hands off" approach.

Because of its purely voluntary nature, the committee turned inward. It decided, for the time being, to bypass problems in education and housing and to concentrate on an area in which the white members could exert some influence — employment.

Two committee members worked on the problem — Robert S. Stevenson, chairman of the Allis-Chalmers Manufacturing Co., and L. B. (Ted) Smith, president of the A. O. Smith Corp. Over the telephone, at lunch and social functions, and in letters, the two men rounded up a group of their friends and acquaintances. Among them were board chairmen and presidents of manufacturing firms, department stores, banks, and other businesses and industries.

Out of their efforts came the formation, on December 16, 1963, of an organization with the mouth filling title of the Milwaukee Voluntary Equal Employment Opportunity Council (MVEEOC). Elmer L. Winter, president of Manpower, Inc., an international temporary help firm, was elected chairman.

Most of the 32 original member companies already had nondiscriminatory hiring policies — or at least said they had. The others, if they had no specific policy, at least had no stated objection to hiring qualified Negroes.

Like We — Milwaukeeans, MVEEOC was organized with a policy of nonintervention. The only requirement for membership was for a company to adopt a written policy of nondiscrimination in hiring, training, promotion, and compensation. Members also were required to use the phrase, "equal opportunity employer," in all employment advertising.

But the requirements ended there. MVEEOC had no specific requirements on how to carry out a policy of nondiscrimination. It did no policing, required no reports. Everything was voluntary and on the honor system. And the stress was on the hiring of qualified members of minority groups. No businessman, said MVEEOC, could be expected to hire anyone who did not meet the requirements for a job. The idea that many job qualifications themselves might be unrealistic, or that businesses and industries might have a responsibility for doing more than opening their doors, was not part of the philosophy then.

Some company presidents in MVEEOC were aware that a company policy might have little or no effect on a personnel supervisor who thought Negroes would disrupt his white work force. So the council conducted seminars for personnel and industrial relations officers of the member companies to allay their suspicions and fears about hiring members of minority groups.

The MVEEOC idea, as far as it went, worked reasonably well. By 1967, the membership had grown to 225 companies in the Milwaukee area, and MVEEOC had set up an office with a part-time executive director. Where earlier there had been no way of determining how effective the organization was, the council by then was producing general statistics on the increases in minority group employment. A Negro who qualified for a job under traditional standards could usually find a job. Soon companies were complaining that they were willing to hire Negroes but could find none who were qualified. The supply of "instant Negroes" ran out quickly.

The formation of the Committee of We — Milwaukeeans and MVEEOC in late 1963 were positive steps in the right direction. Editorial writers, aware of the potential, hailed them. Whether the potential would be realized was another question. But at least there was movement.

Another movement was afoot that summer of 1963. It was a movement that would occupy the civil rights spotlight in Milwaukee for more than two years. It would take the attention from the Social Development Commission and focus it on a much broader and more complicated issue — the existence of in fact, or de facto, segregation in the Milwaukee public schools. The movement would go under the name of the Milwaukee United School Integration Committee. Its struggle would be the second phase in the development of civil rights protests in Milwaukee.

VI

MUSIC FOR MILWAUKEE

They were an unlikely team in 1964 — a 38-year-old Negro attorney and a 39-year-old white woman, a former Catholic nun. But they held center stage in Milwaukee's civil rights movement for nearly two years with school boycotts, sit-ins, and civil disobedience. The issue was de facto segregation in the city's public schools and the target was the Milwaukee School Board.

Lloyd A. Barbee, the attorney, was a relative newcomer to Milwaukee, as was Miss Marilyn J. Morheuser, the former Catholic nun. Barbee, a native of Memphis, Tennessee, moved to Milwaukee in 1962 from Madison, where he had received his law degree in 1956. In Madison, he had worked as a legal consultant to the governor's commission on human rights and had served as chairman of the mayor's commission on human rights.

A slight, courteous man with a taste for cultural pursuits (Shakespeare, cello and viola recitals), Barbee brought an intellectual approach to the Milwaukee civil rights movement. This did not, however, keep him from making blistering, often bitter, public attacks on members of the school board, the mayor, or other public officials, using words like "nincompoop" and "phony liberal."

It was Barbee who, as chairman of the Wisconsin conference of branches of the NAACP in 1963, first raised the issue of de facto school segregation with the Milwaukee School Board. The issue

50

actually was brought up before the CORE protest against the membership of Fred Lins on the Social Development Commission, but it did not gather steam until the next year.

It was a time when most people had never heard of de facto segregation, when newspapers in Milwaukee defined the term every time they used it. The usual definition was "racial separation of student populations in fact if not in law, not necessarily intentional, and often the result of housing patterns."

The school board responded by appointing a new Committee on Equality of Educational Opportunity — a committee which was to become a source of frustration to the city's civil rights organizations and many other well-meaning individuals and organizations who wanted to get something done about a school system that was, in fact, segregated.

All of Milwaukee's civil rights organizations and responsible Negro leaders lined up against the school board on the issue, but it was basically an NAACP campaign, with strong support from the Milwaukee CORE chapter. CORE provided the bodies for direct action in the early months of the protest by picketing some of the schools.

In December, 1963, Barbee presented an 80-page report to the special committee, headed by Harold W. Story, a gruff, white-haired attorney with a penchant for legalism. Its basic premise was that de facto segregated schools were inherently inferior. But it also said that whites were handicapped by segregation in their understanding of reality and in their social relations. These two areas, the report said, were fundamental problems of child development for which schools were responsible.

At the time, school officials kept no statistics on the racial makeup of the public schools, adhering to what they called a "color blind" policy. The NAACP said it had conducted its own survey and found that one high school, two junior high schools, and 11 elementary schools were more than 90 percent Negro. Four other elementary schools, it said, were 60 to 90 percent Negro, and there were two high schools, a junior high school, and four elementary schools which were about 50 percent Negro.

The approach to the special committee was moderate, although the proposals were radical at the time. And Barbee did tell the committee members that the NAACP would engage in direct action unless the school board took definite steps to alleviate de facto segregation. Among the suggestions he made were establishing a clear-cut policy for integrating the schools, allowing Negro students to transfer into white schools, re-zoning neighborhood school districts to bring more Negro students into schools that had high white enrollments, building new schools in locations that would assure integration, and assigning Negro teachers, recreation workers, and administrators throughout the city.

Two weeks later, Story commented: "As I read their report, it would abolish the neighborhood school system as it operates here."

From then on, preservation of the neighborhood school system at all costs became the guiding principle of the majority of the special committee and the majority of the school board. It remained that way at the end of 1967.

The special committee went through the motions of "studying" the problems of Milwaukee's inner core schools. In reality, the majority of the committee members showed, in their discussions at committee meetings and in public statements, that their minds were made up to preserve the status quo. Often, instead of discussing a proposal made by a responsible organization or individual, majority members of the committee would seek to discredit the organization or minimize the influence of the individual. For example, when the Greater Milwaukee Conference on Religion and Race, whose members included Milwaukee's leading clergymen, asked the school board to take action on the issue, Miss Lorraine Radtke said sarcastically that the clergymen did not really represent the views of members of their congregations.

Miss Radtke, then the school board president and a member of the special committee, also put together a one-sided "Bibliographical Digest" to guide the school board on civil rights matters. The digest was loaded with materials intended to buttress the school board majority's position.

The issue produced a deep split between the majority and minority factions on the school board and the special committee, to the point where the two factions had ceased to communicate. The minority faction tried to get the majority to go along with various proposals, some of them so innocuous that they would have required nothing more than a nod. All were rejected. The majority of the committee and the board refused even to recognize that de facto segregation existed.

Soon there was complete estrangement between the school board and the civil rights organizations. In March, 1964, the state NAACP and the Milwaukee CORE chapter formed the Milwaukee United School Integration Committee, with Barbee as chairman. It was organized for the express purpose of conducting a boycott of Milwaukee's Negro area public schools.

Miss Morheuser, who had worked with Barbee in the state NAACP, became secretary of the new committee, the acronym for which was MUSIC. In 1963, Miss Morheuser had received a papal dispensation from her vows as a Sister of Loretto at the Foot of the Cross, an order which had its headquarters in Nerinx, Kentucky. She left the order, she said, because she had found the religious life too confining for her expanding interest in civil rights. Miss Morheuser had done graduate work in journalism at Milwaukee's Marquette University, and after leaving the order she became editor of the *Milwaukee Star,* a weekly Negro newspaper.

Miss Morheuser was a tireless worker with a strong streak of emotionalism that was in marked contrast to Barbee's calculated approach to the situation. She became Barbee's right arm on the committee. But there were others, too: The Rev. B. S. Gregg, the friendly and optimistic pastor of St. Matthew Christian Methodist Episcopal Church, who provided the financial backbone and headquarters space for MUSIC in his church; Thomas M. Jacobson, an ambitious young German-born Jewish attorney who was Barbee's law partner; John H. Givens, Jr., the CORE chapter chairman who had led the demonstrations against Fred Lins; Cecil Brown, Jr., an articulate former state assemblyman with a talent for rubbing some people the wrong way; E. Gordon Young, a law student who later was to become an assistant attorney general; and Leslie Johnson, the quiet and hard working vice-chairman of the Milwaukee CORE chapter.

Some CORE chapter members were hesitant about the boycott because they doubted whether there was enough support in the black community to conduct one successfully. However, after a rally at Mr. Gregg's church at which about 350 persons, many of them parents of schoolchildren, expressed nearly unanimous support for the boycott, CORE voted to support it.

Before the rally, the CORE chapter already had been actively involved in the school issue. Chapter members had picketed schools to protest the school board's "intact busing" policy.

Under the policy, when schools became overcrowded or were closed down for remodeling, children were transported by bus to other schools. White as well as Negro children were bused, but the majority of the classes were Negro. The United States Commission on Civil Rights, in its 1967 report, *Racial Isolation in the Public Schools,* described the situation:

In Milwaukee, the school system had bused white children for many years, picking them up near their homes, returning them at the end of the day, and almost invariably integrating them into classes at the receiving school. The practice changed in 1957 when the school system began busing Negro children to predominantly white schools. The Negro children were kept in separate classrooms at the receiving schools. They also were returned home for lunch even when the receiving schools had lunchroom facilities. In one instance, a number of Negro children lived closer to their white receiving school than to the Negro sending school where they were enrolled officially. They were nonetheless required to walk to the sending school to board the bus. If the boundary had been changed, these children could have been enrolled officially in the school to which they were bused as a group and then could have walked to their neighborhood school.

The practice of keeping separate the Negro children who are bused has continued in Milwaukee but now Negro pupils are permitted to remain at the receiving schools for lunch. After proposals were made to integrate the bused children fully into the receiving schools on an experimental basis, the board declared busing to be educationally undesirable and discontinued busing children from two majority-Negro schools.

To members of the civil rights organizations and many other Negroes and whites who favored integration, the intact busing issue was the most flagrant and visible example of the school board's determination to maintain a segregated school system.

The reaction of Milwaukee's white majority to the announcement of the school boycott was typical of its reaction to every civil rights protest before and since. Instead of focusing on the issue the boycott was intended to dramatize, the boycott itself became the issue. People said it was illegal, the children would be harmed by being kept out of school, the civil rights organizations were "using" children, the boycott leaders should be arrested and thrown in jail. There were even, as always, a few Negroes who actively and publicly denounced the boycott.

Story slammed the door on the civil rights integration proposals on April 24. The only proposal that the school board could legally meet, he said, would be an open enrollment policy. A free transfer policy already existed under which pupils could transfer from their own schools into schools with openings — if they had a good reason. A desire for integration was not considered a good reason, although a white parent's desire to get his child out of a predominantly Negro school apparently had been. Under an open enrollment policy, a transfer would be permitted for any reason.

Story said that all of the other integration proposals would require the school board to consider race in setting policies. "What the NAACP is asking for is in complete violation of the law," he said. "It's almost sacred in our democratic concept of things that we do things without reference to race, religion and all the other things."

A proposal to have the school board adopt a policy statement favoring integration, Story said, would only be words. "Those words have got to be interpreted," he said, "and then you can have an argument. So what if you do have a silly statement of policy? The problems of the central city are still going to be there. Let's go to work on those problems."

Three days after the May 18 school boycott, Story's committee adopted open enrollment, along with a policy statement declaring that "The hope of short- and long-term accomplishment for central city schools lies in massive compensatory education." All other proposals, plans, and arguments were rejected.

The school board later adopted the committee's recommendation. It was the only concession the board made. Neighborhood schools, which had become a shibboleth for resistance to integration proposals, were safe. Nearly four years later, at the end of 1967, the situation had not changed.

Because the boycott itself became the issue, there were attempts to head it off. The most notable of these was a request for a postponement from Mayor Maier. The mayor offered the services of his office in bringing the Milwaukee school board and boycott leaders together to seek "a better public understanding of the points at issue, upon which there apparently is much confusion."

The mayor expressed fear that the boycott could result in harm to the city. It could, he said, undo in one day the work of many months in which more Milwaukeeans had been enrolled in efforts to attain interracial justice than ever before. The reference apparently was to the new Committee of We — Milwaukeeans.

Maier proposed establishment of an impartial panel to serve as a moderator. If not that, he said, MUSIC and the school board each could name one panel member with the two of them naming the third. A better public understanding of the issues would be the least result of such a meeting, Maier said.

It was a moderate proposal, which eventually might have produced some break in the impasse. MUSIC accepted the mediation offer, although members declined to postpone the boycott as the mayor had asked. But the school board was in no mood to budge an inch. Three days before the boycott, the board rejected the mayor's proposal by a 9 to 6 vote. The board also voted down a proposal that it adopt a statement recognizing "the racial imbalance that exists in our core area schools." Oddly enough, the motion was introduced by one of the more conservative members of the board, one who had become identified with the majority faction. When the roll call came, however, he did not even vote for his own motion. He voted "present."

Civil rights issues in those early months of 1964 were sharpened by the appearance on the Milwaukee scene of an apostle of segregation from the south, George Corley Wallace, governor of Alabama and White House hopeful. In speeches during his Milwaukee campaign, Wallace hammered away at the Civil Rights Acts of 1964, then pending in Congress. Although he did not mention the de facto segregation issue in the city specifically, part of his theme was that the Civil Rights Act would take away the rights of citizens to run their own school systems.

The Alabama governor took 31.3 percent of the Milwaukee vote in the presidential primary. He said if he ever had to leave Alabama, "I'd want to live on the south side of Milwaukee."

Wallace's campaign was a sidelight in the school segregation issue. For a short time, it diverted some attention from the impending school boycott, as members of civil rights organizations spent some of their energies picketing the governor's hotel and buildings where he made speeches and appearances.

Perhaps the most noteworthy thing about the Wallace campaign, from a civil rights standpoint, was that it marked the first time that clergymen participated publicly in civil rights demonstrations in Milwaukee. Eight Catholic priests and about ten Catholic seminarians, led by Father Matthew Gottschalk, were among the Wallace pickets. Father Matthew, a Capuchin priest, was the pastor of St. Francis Church, a parish in the heart of the city's black ghetto. Optimistic, strong, yet quiet, he was every inch a man's man who saw light in the darkness of Milwaukee's inner core. "It all depends what you're looking for," he once said. "If you're looking for frustrations or intrigued by the moral aberrations of which man is capable, you will find them in abundance. But if you can brush aside the clinging cobwebs of surface imperfections, you will also find a variety of richness of human goodness that will help to balance off the ominous sociological studies of the ghetto."

At the time, the appearance of a clergyman on a picket line — particularly a bearded Capuchin priest wearing sandals and brown robe — was something of a curiosity. Few Milwaukeeans paid any attention to it. But it was inkling of the increased public involvement of clergymen in civil rights issues that was yet to come, an involvement that was to reach its emotional peak exactly one year later in the city of Selma in Governor Wallace's state of Alabama. Father Matthew would be one of those clergymen in Selma, along with other Milwaukee residents, including a priest most Milwaukeeans had never heard of — Father James Edward Groppi.

Milwaukee's first school boycott came off, as scheduled, on May 18, 1964 — the tenth anniversary of the United States Supreme Court's historic decision in *Brown v. Board of Education,* which outlawed what had been legal school segregation in the south. The boycott was well-planned and well-executed. The boycott committee set up 31 Freedom Schools for children who stayed away from classes in the public schools.

Most of them were in small Negro churches, but one of them was in All Saints Cathedral, the home parish of the Episcopal bishop of Milwaukee, Donald H. V. Hallock. Miss Morheuser had spent months recruiting teachers for the Freedom Schools and, on the day of the boycott, there were 320 of them. They included students, businessmen, retired teachers, clergymen, college professors, professionals, blue collar workers, and even a few public school teachers. Mothers of children who stayed out of school served as chefs and chauffeurs, and a few of them taught.

The churches had new names for the day. Crispus Attucks School, JFK School, Martin Luther King School, Marian Anderson School, Frederick Douglass Senior High School, and James Baldwin School were some of the names.

Miss Morheuser, along with other MUSIC members, also worked out elaborate curricula for the schools. There were discussions of freedom, brotherhood, the boycott, equality, and justice. Studies centered around Negro history, racial myths, and human relations. Teachers were urged to "help students understand that the withdrawal is not a rebellion against schools, teachers, principals or authority, but rather an organized, orderly, united effort to get better schools."

The boycott went off without a hitch. *The Milwaukee Journal* editorialized: "Whatever may have been the wisdom of the school boycott Monday, the conduct of it was splendid. It was well-organized and well-controlled. It testifies to the amount of basic goodwill in the community that not a single disorderly incident was reported. The demonstration of this point may have been its best effect."

Harold S. Vincent, superintendent of the Milwaukee public schools, reported that the number of pupils absent from 30 Negro area schools on the day of the boycott was 11,138 greater than on the previous Monday. Barbee disputed the figures. He said that the total difference was closer to 15,000 absent from 28 schools that MUSIC said were segregated.

At the time, there was a total of 115,080 pupils in the city's public schools. Of that number, 91,224 were white and 23,856 were nonwhite. (Although the school administration kept no statistics on racial breakdowns when the school dispute started, it conducted a "head count" early in 1964.)

In its editorial on the boycott, the *Journal* accused the school board majority of displaying an "aggressive stubbornness" in spurning Mayor Maier's efforts to act as an intermediary between the board and the civil rights organizations. Then the editorial asked: "So where do we go from here? Through more months of quibbling legalism, to the point where prolonged inaction will have to be viewed as actual stalling? Into another school year under conditions likely to provoke more demonstrations under greater tensions. . . .?"

The questions were prophetic. The school board majority remained rigid, with the exception of its adoption of the open enrollment policy. Miss Radtke, the school board president, set the tone in speeches and public statements in which she contended again and again that what she called "forced integration" could not take place. She also assailed clergymen for their increasing involvement in social issues. It was not their responsibility, she said, to act as a "political bloc."

In a speech in June, 1964, to members of the Milwaukee Ministerial Association, she said she would like to see Negroes develop a course of their own. "I would like to see him excel," she said "in areas which have not been thoroughly developed by white people. I think that the Negro has a great deal to offer our culture in the fields of the arts — music, drama, painting and sports. He should develop his skills to the utmost. He should be original in his approach to living. He should realize that he need not imitate the white man to fulfill his culture."

Curiously enough, Miss Radtke's words also proved prophetic, but not in the way she and others like her would have wanted. Negroes in 1967 began developing a "course of their own." It went under the name of Black Power, and in many cities — not in Milwaukee — black power militants advocated some of the same things that Miss Radtke and other members of the school board, in their shortsightedness, also advocated. In Detroit, for example, black power groups no longer favored integration. Instead, they were asking for massive doses of compensatory education for black ghetto schools.

The black power concept, in many ways, is a healthy one. But where it is a specter that strikes fear into the hearts of whites, it is partly a result of the stereotyped, myopic attitudes of the Miss Radtkes and others like her all over the country.

Civil rights activity in Milwaukee in the aftermath of its first school boycott was relatively quiet. Civil rights organizations continued to protest the school board's inaction by picketing meetings of the special committee and the board itself. But they might as well have been picketing in Phoenix, for all the effect they had.

During the summer, the Milwaukee CORE chapter began its slow decline into oblivion. A split developed within the chapter over whether it should withdraw from the Milwaukee United School Integration Committee. Givens, the chapter chairman, wanted out. CORE, he said, would lose its identity if it continued as a member of the boycott committee. Besides, he contended, the committee had accomplished what it set out to do by conducting the May 18 school boycott.

The opposition to Givens was led by Cecil Brown, then vice-chairman of CORE, who favored continued membership in MUSIC. The split became so bitter that national CORE officials placed the chapter under a trusteeship. Later the members themselves voted to dissolve the chapter, but the national office would not sanction the move.

When the smoke had cleared, Givens and most of his supporters had left the chapter, and Brown was left as de facto head of the organization. Later he was elected chairman. But much of the chapter's vitality was gone, and it declined in influence. Finally, after another scrap among the remaining members in October, 1967, the national office dissolved the chapter.

The latter part of 1964 and early 1965 were periods of relative calm in the Milwaukee civil rights movement. During the former, the nation's attention was riveted on Lyndon B. Johnson's first campaign for election to the presidency against Barry Goldwater. During the latter, the nation's attention was focused southward on the Selma voting rights drive of the Rev. Martin Luther King, Jr., and his Southern Christian Leadership Conference.

Selma disturbed the conscience of the nation, particularly after the Rev. James Reeb, a white Unitarian minister from Boston, was fatally beaten for having the temerity to eat in a Negro restaurant there. Clergymen, nuns, and other civil rights advocates from all over the nation traveled there to provide a witness of Christian, Jewish, and even atheist concern over the plight of their black brothers in the southern city.

Selma touched Milwaukee, too. Five priests, two Catholic nuns, and two ministers were among the early Milwaukee representatives in the demonstrations. Besides Fathers Groppi and Matthew Gottschalk, they were Msgr. Franklyn J. Kennedy, editorial manager of the *Catholic Herald Citizen* of Milwaukee (there to function as a newsman, not a demonstrator); Father Patrick Flood, then an assistant at St. Thomas Aquinas Church; Father Austin Schlaefer, an assistant at St. Elizabeth's Church; the Rev. Richard Aukema, pastor of Christ Presbyterian Church; the Rev. Christopher Raible, minister of the Unitarian Church West; Sister Mary Jeanine, head of the sociology department at Cardinal Stritch College, and Sister Ann Frances, a sociology instructor at St. Mary's Academy.

Although Msgr. Kennedy was in Selma only as an observer, he had long fought for civil rights causes. Shortly after World War II, he led the battle to desegregate the American Bowling Congress, which had a whites-only membership policy. At 60, he was enjoying his role as newsman and interpreter of the Selma demonstrations for Milwaukee's Catholics. Needless to say, his stories and editorials reflected his strong civil rights convictions. A little more than two years after the Selma demonstrations, on June 3, 1967, he died of cancer.

The Selma demonstrations resembled a massive religious retreat. Msgr. Kennedy, as well as others, sensed it. A highly emotional sense of brotherhood and well-being pervaded the George Washington

Carver Housing Project, where the demonstrations centered. It was the high point of the nonviolent, integrated civil rights movement. The movement crashed in flames the following August in an area of the City of Los Angeles called Watts.

But Selma was a time for self-examination, particularly for the clergymen. Some of those who thought about it found that they were suffering from a moral dichotomy, demonstrating their concern several hundred, even a thousand, miles from home but not demonstrating that same concern in their own back yards. For many of the clergymen and nuns, it was a turning point, and northern cities began to see increasing numbers of men and women in clerical garb on picket lines and in other demonstrations.

The Milwaukeeans were no exception. After his return from Selma, Father Groppi joined the Milwaukee United School Integration Committee and later was elected second vice-chairman of the organization. The rest of the clergymen, along with others who had not traveled to the Selma demonstrations, became active participants in the Milwaukee civil rights struggle.

In May and June of 1965, the integration committee conducted a series of demonstrations against the school board's policy of keeping Negro children in separate classes after busing them to white schools. MUSIC members, using automobiles like a civil rights Afrika Korps, kept police on the run by popping up at different schools without warning, then picketing or blocking school buses by forming human chains in front of them. Often reporters and television cameramen would be at the scene of a demonstration before the police arrived.

Barbee was among the first of dozens of MUSIC members arrested during the protest. It was during this series of demonstrations that Father Groppi experienced his first civil rights arrest. On June 4, Father Groppi and four other clergymen formed a human chain by linking their arms in front of a school bus at the Siefert Elementary School. The others were Father William J. Miles, rector of St. George's Episcopal Church, an inner core parish less than a block from St. Boniface; the Rev. Lucius Walker, executive director of Northcott Neighborhood House, a Methodist agency; the Rev. L. T. King, assistant pastor of Tabernacle Community Baptist Church, and the Rev. Gregg, the treasurer of the integration committee. Each later was fined $10 for blocking traffic.

At the time, Father Groppi was just a name among other names, one of a group of clergymen arrested in a civil rights protest. Most Milwaukeeans still had not heard of him. His only previous public mention had been as one of the group of clergymen and nuns from Milwaukee who participated in the Selma demonstrations. He had not yet reached the point where the very mention of his name could produce instant emotional responses ranging from affection to rage.

On the third day after his arrest, however, Father Groppi indicated what his future attitude toward civil rights issues was to be. At a rally at the St. Matthew CME Church, he said: "I believe a clergyman's place is with his people. There have been ten of my parishioners who submitted themselves to arrest to point out what they believe to be an injustice. . . . I believe that a person must work in the orderly procedures of society to bring about social justice. But when the orderly procedures do not bring man his rights in society, then a man can go beyond these orderly procedures. . . . Every means possible has been used, in my estimation, to move the school board to take some action. The children have been integrated in other cities where this intact busing has taken place."

Separation, Father Groppi said, increases race consciousness. At the time, it was considered sound principle for civil rights militants to try to get programs that would rid Negroes and whites of race consciousness. That, of course, was before the new black awareness. Father Groppi himself, a few years later, would be doing everything he could to increase race consciousness, especially racial pride among black people.

The intact busing issue was one on which school officials could, in my view and in that of others, have acted with relative ease. It would not have been difficult to integrate classes at the host schools. There might have been a bit more paper work, but integrating the classes would have at least shown Negroes in Milwaukee that there was some sensitivity on the school board and among top school administrators toward the city's visible minority.

But Harold S. Vincent, the superintendent of schools, said it was "administratively unfeasible" to integrate the classes. The school board nodded, and that was that. No one except the civil rights militants even questioned whether it was feasible.

If an attempt had been made to integrate the classes, it is quite likely that there would have been vicious protests from parents of the white children at the receiving schools. It also is likely that the school board majority and Vincent were aware of this possibility. And if there is anything the school board and school officials displayed during these times it was sensitivity toward the feelings of the white majority.

At the time, Vincent perhaps could have exerted some influence on the school board. As a top school administrator, he was not unaware of the implications of the de facto school segregation issue. But, at 64, he was nearing the end of his career and chose a passive role instead of an active one, responding to and defending the school board instead of attempting to lead it. (Vincent died of a heart attack July 10, 1968, a little more than a year after his retirement.)

The school bus demonstrations, abetted by sit-ins of CORE members at the school administration building, produced the usual response. The majority of Milwaukee area residents paid little attention; there was no threat to them. Again the criticism was of the civil rights tactics, not of the school board or the school administration. Two judges, who handled the cases of some of the demonstrators, even felt compelled to defend the school board in statements from the bench. County Judge John E. Krueger told demonstrators that they should not try to coerce the school board. A former school board member himself, Judge Krueger said that no one could ever say that the board did not give "each situation a chance to be heard." County Judge Christ T. Seraphim also praised the school board and told several of the demonstrators: "You can't get civil rights by doing civil wrongs."

Judges in Milwaukee are political animals who must stand for reelection every few years. And in Milwaukee, opposition to the civil rights movement is good politics, while civil rights advocacy is political suicide. This is why public officials sometimes go out of their way to criticize civil rights tactics, as Judge Seraphim did two days after the May 18 school boycott.

The case involved a 27-year-old Negro woman, the mother of seven children, six of them illegitimate. She was convicted of prostitution. The case had nothing to do with the public school boycott, nothing to do with the issues involved. The only connections, none of them legitimate, were that she was a Negro, she came into court while the boycott was still fresh in the judge's mind, and her attorney's brother had been involved in some of the boycott planning.

But this was enough to elicit irrelevant, gratuitous comments from Judge Seraphim. He called the boycott a "goofy stunt" and said he should place the prostitute on probation to the boycott leaders. Why?

ᴶBecause Judge Seraphim thought that the boycott leaders, instead of running boycotts, should be counseling parents so parents would motivate their children to stay out of trouble and maybe wind up being solid middle-class citizens instead of prostitutes and criminals and things like that.

But Milwaukee had not seen its last school boycott. While the school bus demonstrations were still in progress, the integration committee leaders already were discussing a second boycott. Even before the school bus demonstrations had started, Barbee — by then he had been elected as the only Negro in the state assembly — had announced publicly that MUSIC planned a boycott that would surpass "in both scope and duration" any boycott ever conducted in the United States.

Barbee was not a man to leave any bases uncovered. He had approached the school board with a study, had participated in discussions, had walked out on Story's Committee, had blocked school buses, conducted a boycott and had another boycott cooking. But to make sure all the avenues were covered, in June of 1965, he filed a federal court suit on behalf of a group of Negro and white parents of schoolchildren. The suit charged the Milwaukee school board with operating a segregated school system. It received the backing of the national NAACP organization, which had a tradition of fighting legal battles for civil rights.

Preparation of the case against the school board involved painstaking gathering of records and other data. Because of this, the suit had not yet come to trial by the summer of 1968.

But the suit was the long-range shot. For the immediate protest, MUSIC had its second school boycott to look forward to. In September, Barbee announced that the boycott would start on October 18, exactly a year and a half after the first boycott, and would go on indefinitely. Again the reaction was swift: MUSIC had made its point; why have another boycott? They're using children. It's illegal. And so on.

Again there were the requests for cancellation and postponement, from the mayor and others. The first request came from Henry S. Reuss, the Democratic congressman whose district included Milwaukee's inner core. Reuss reacted after three members of the school board proposed a pilot program to integrate Negro children bused to white schools into classes at the host schools. He asked the boycott leaders to temporarily suspend plans for the boycott, and at the same time asked the school board to act promptly on the integration experiment.

But the effort was doomed to failure. Two members of the committee on equality of educational opportunity, who represented the minority on the school board that was willing to take some action, tried to get their committee to meet on the experimental program. But they could not even get other committee members to show up for meetings they called.

Meanwhile the school board was deluged with statements, proposals, and letters from religious, academic, civic, political, and labor organizations. The communications varied, but all asked the board, in some way, to take steps to alleviate the problem of de facto segregation, or racial imbalance, in the public schools. It all fell on deaf ears. The majority of the school board, although it officially still refused to recognize the existence of the problem, had begun to talk about it informally. The new line of argument by this time was that de facto segregation was caused by housing patterns, the school board was not responsible for housing patterns, and, therefore, the school board had no responsibility to try to help solve the problem.

By then, the presidency of the school board had changed hands, from Miss Radtke to Attorney John F. Foley, but the sounds Foley made when he talked were exactly like those Miss Radtke had made when she was president. When he assumed the presidency, one of Foley's first acts was to reappoint Story as chairman of the Committee on Equality of Educational Opportunity. He also adamantly defended the neighborhood school system, insisting that any school integration had to come through changes in housing patterns. Referring to the boycott, Foley said that the school board "would not be coerced into establishing board policy by threats of any kind and in particular an illegal act."

The two sides became rooted in place; the boycott committee would not call off the boycott unless the school board took positive action to relieve de facto segregation, and the school board would take no action under the threat of a boycott. Nor, for that matter, would the school board take any action without the threat of a boycott. It had proved that for more than two years.

Action had to come from somewhere else. And it did. Ten days before the boycott was to begin, the Committee of We — Milwaukeeans, which had largely been dormant since formation of the Milwaukee Voluntary Equal Employment Opportunity Council, proposed a complete study of the Milwaukee public school system, to be financed 50-50 by the school board and We — Milwaukeeans.

The main reason for the study proposal, of course, was the de facto school segregation issue. But to get the school board to swallow the study, it could not simply concentrate on that issue. Besides, the entire school system did need studying.

Considerable pressure apparently was put on some school board members to get them to vote for the study proposal. The proposal sailed right through the special committee and, later, the board itself. There seemed to be no question of whether the board members would vote for the study; the only questions were over procedures and goals.

Later, when Foley hit the front pages in a bitter attack on some of the study findings that were prematurely released, the assistant dean of the school of education at a large university remarked: "The Milwaukee school board apparently is in the position of getting a study it doesn't want." Indeed, it may have been that some school board members voted for the study in the belief that it would vindicate their positions that de facto segregation was not a school board responsibility. But the majority of the board did find itself with a study that ended up diametrically opposed to their stand on the issue.

After We — Milwaukeeans proposed the study, Mayor Maier used the proposal as the basis for asking Barbee and the members of MUSIC to call off the boycott. The mayor called the study proposal "a tremendous breakthrough in this long standing problem." But to Barbee and the committee members, it was another eleventh-hour way of trying to get the boycott called off. "I consider the two fighting words in the inner core, in dealing with human rights problems, are 'committee' and 'study,' " Barbee said. "These two words themselves are insulting to the people who are fighting for human rights."

Throughout the de facto segregation controversy, the mayor had refrained from criticizing the school board or involving himself in the actual issue. He contended that the mayor had no jurisdiction over school problems.

He had no jurisdiction over the civil rights organizations, either, but this did not prevent him from lecturing them. After Barbee refused to call off the boycott as the mayor requested, Maier wrote him a letter expressing his disappointment. He also defined what the "real battles" were in the civil rights movement in Milwaukee.

The mayor said that the fight for equal opportunity in the city required constant battles on many fronts, including a fight for more revenues for Milwaukee — a city that "is more discriminated against fiscally than any other city in the state" — greater educational facilities, and a constant program against discrimination.

"These are battles," Maier said, "which are all related to the question of opportunity in Milwaukee, including that of equality of education, since here, too, Milwaukee must fight its battles alone, cut off from the resources of the metropolitan area, just as 98 percent of the area's Negroes are cut off from residency in the most segregated suburbs of any metropolitan area in the country. My contention is that many of the good efforts that are being made may be washed away by an overriding public image of the boycott tactic. Further, the boycott pits internal forces against each other within the central city, while the real battle with the segregated suburbs goes unattended."

Needless to say, the mayor's lecture went unheeded by the civil rights leaders. Then, five days before the boycott, the mayor introduced his grand program for solving Milwaukee's civil rights problems. It was a campaign to show that "prejudice and discrimination are as un-American as Communism." It was Mayor Maier's "War on Prejudice."

The proposal had a high sound to it — sort of like coming out with a program to promote patriotism, love of mother, and reverence for the American flag. Who could be against a program to stamp out prejudice and discrimination? A lot of Milwaukeeans could be for such a program and still not want to have anything to do with Negroes. Besides, the mayor did not say anything about blacks living with or going to school with whites. And he did criticize the civil rights organizations for making noisy efforts that were not meaningful.

The mayor asked the Milwaukee Commission on Community relations — perhaps the most inept organization in the city in terms of accomplishing what it was supposed to do — to set up an advisory council to plan a full year's program for the "War on Prejudice." The advisory council was to have been composed of representatives of the communications industries, professional producers, writers, directors, public relations men, psychologists, educators, and other professional people.

The Community Relations Commission was the city's official agency set up to handle problems of human rights. It depended on the common council of the city for money, and on the mayor for members

— commissioners were mayoral appointees. The commission's chief contribution to the advancement of community relations in the city was that it had succeeded in hardly ever offending anybody.

Eventually, the commission contracted for a study of the problem. The city paid $25,000 for "A Plan to Reduce Prejudice and Discrimination in the Milwaukee Area." And the city got gypped. The Greenleigh Report, as it was known around city hall, resembled something a sophomore liberal arts student might put together with a bit of research in the public library. The report consisted of generalizations, inaccuracies, and recommendations based on them. Even so, some of the recommendations were not bad.

But in early 1968, two and one-half years after the mayor declared his "War on Prejudice," the first shot had yet to be fired.

The public school boycott of October, 1965, lasted three and one-half days. From a numbers standpoint, none of the days proved as successful — from the civil rights side — as the boycott in May, 1964. School absences ranged from 4,100 more than usual to about 7,300 more than the average daily absences for the previous month. But the boycott was, up to that time, the longest in the country.

Again MUSIC set up Freedom Schools for the boycotting pupils, and again there were demonstrations accompanying the boycott. Barbee and the mayor had a biting exchange of words in the daily newspapers after the mayor accused some of the civil rights demonstrators of "Ku Klux Klanism in reverse." The mayor's comment referred to picketing of the home of Foley, the school board president, by about 265 children and teen-agers, most of them Negroes.

Because of his comment, the mayor himself was the target of picketing the following night. More than 300 pickets, again mostly high school students, walked quietly in front of the apartment building in which the mayor lived. The next day, Maier accused Barbee of making a personal attack on him. Then he proceeded to make a personal attack on Barbee. He said Barbee was a "pettifogger" who made speeches and organized children for late night marches instead of responsibly seeking progress in his cause.

Barbee responded by saying that the mayor's leadership in civil rights "speaks for itself and it ranges from a mere whisper to a whining whimper." He also referred to the War on Prejudice as a "phony Madison Avenue" phrase, and said Milwaukee's Negro population was worse off under Maier's two administrations than at any other time before.

The school boycott received nation-wide attention, but it was not because the mayor and Barbee spent part of their time squaring off at each other. The publicity came about because a group of Catholic priests in the inner city decided to support the school boycott by lending the use of their parish buildings as Freedom Schools. About 25 priests were involved, including the four who had been in Selma — Fathers Groppi, Gottschalk, Flood, and Schlaefer. Most directly involved, however, were the pastors of the five inner city Catholic parishes.

On October 7, eleven days before the boycott was scheduled to begin, priests of the five parishes announced that they would conduct Freedom Schools. Their decision stood unchallenged for nearly a week. Archdiocesan officials, Father Groppi said, "trust us to act in whatever way we see fit."

But they did not. Starting on October 14, and for the next three days, the priests and archdiocesan officialdom became involved in a comedy of errors based on assumptions and inadequate communication.

It started with an order from Monsignor Edmund J. Goebel, the archdiocesan superintendent of schools. In it, he forbade participation in boycott activities by Catholic pastors and school principals. The immediate reaction of many of the priests was that the monsignor had no authority to dictate their personal activities.

For some reason, Msgr. Goebel made no mention of the school buildings themselves. The question then became whether the buildings might be used for Freedom Schools with someone other than the priests operating them.

Unfortunately, Archbishop William E. Cousins was out of the city at the time, attending the Vatican Council in Rome. Left in charge of the archdiocese was Roman R. Atkielski, the auxiliary bishop, who, instead of clearing up the situation, regrettably further confused it.

Bishop Atkielski issued an order that almost exactly reversed the order that Msgr. Goebel had sent out. The bishop prohibited the use of parish facilities for Freedom Schools, but left up in the air the question of participation in the boycott by priests and nuns.

The bishop may have assumed that the inner core priests would interpret the order as banning their participation in the boycott. He even said as much to a reporter who asked the question. The order, said Bishop Atkielski, did ban participation by priests and nuns. But

there was no such wording in the bishop's letter to the inner core
pastors, and the priests from the Negro area churches were quite
willing to be literalists about the situation. They assumed nothing
and paid no attention to the statements in the newspapers attributed
to the bishop.

And, because they believed he did not understand their position
in the matter, the priests asked to meet with Bishop Atkielski. But
the bishop said he could see no reason for that because, he said, his
order did not relate to the morality or moral implications of the
boycott. In his letter to the priests, the bishop merely had said that
anyone aiding or abetting parents in keeping their children out of
school would subject himself to prosecution by civil authorities.

Because the bishop was not passing on the morality of participation in the boycott, the priests felt that they had the right to disagree
with him. They did just that in a statement which they cleared with
the bishop over the telephone. The statement, released to the press
— the bishop had not objected to its release — said: "We respect
him (Bishop Atkielski) as holding an office from the hand of Christ.
But it is with sorrow and regret that we declare we do not think
he understands the facts of the situation as they are. Accordingly,
in our own consciences, we do not see his directions, based upon
a legal decision, as morally binding with the force of Christ's words
. . . there is substantial doubt as to the alleged illegality of a public
school boycott. . . . The order of Bishop Atkielski is thus based on
an infirm interpretation of the law."

The fact that the bishop had not objected to the public release of
the statement was interpreted by many of the priests as a victory for
freedom of conscience. Priests of four of the inner core parishes —
St. Boniface, St. Benedict the Moor, St. Francis, and St. Elizabeth
— decided to conduct Freedom Schools in spite of the bishop's order,
believing that their own moral consciousness in this case superseded
the bishop's legal interpretation of the boycott.

"If children turn up at Catholic schools, despite what the bishop
has said, we feel that in conscience we have to take them in rather
than let them run the streets," Father Groppi commented. "We feel
that if the bishop himself were here in the parish, he would open the
doors to them rather than turn them out. That is the only way we can
interpret Christ acting in such circumstances."

But the "victory" for the priests proved to be short-lived. On
Sunday, October 17, the day before the boycott, Msgr. Leo J. Brust,

the chancellor of the archdiocese, told the priests that their statement of disagreement with the bishop was a direct violation of religious authority. The pastors of the four churches reluctantly but obediently closed their parish facilities to the boycotters.

But the pastors felt the need to explain their positions in the matter. To do so, they bought advertising space in Milwaukee's daily newspapers and used it to publish "An Open Letter to Our People." The letter read:

On Saturday evening, Oct. 16, 1965, Bishop Roman R. Atkielski said that our group of interested priests, sisters and lay people were permitted to express our conscientious judgment, which was opposed to the bishop's in the matter of the school boycott and Freedom Schools in Milwaukee.

It was with great joy that we received his statement. We thought that the church in Milwaukee was being given the historic distinction of being the first place in our country where a church authority would apply in a specific case the declaration of freedom of conscience as enunciated just a few weeks ago in Rome by the Second Vatican Ecumenical Council. It seems that we overestimated the situation.

We have been informed through inadequate communication lines by our local curial officials that we are forbidden to allow the parish property and facilities to be used for the Freedom Schools. As priests, servants of our parishes, we were faced with the choice of obeying the bishop, in which case we feel that our church fails to give its full Christian witness here. On the other hand, should we disobey the bishop, we feel that at this time in our church many would not be able to understand our actions, and so would suffer some spiritual harm because they are not yet ready to receive the full impact of Vatican II.

With every protest short of direct disobedience, and with the conviction that we are substantially betraying our people, but with the hope that we have not done so, we revert to the basic training we have been given and reluctantly closed our parish facilities to the use of the Freedom Schools.

The signers were Father Eugene F. Bleidorn, pastor of St. Boniface, Father Earl Goeden of St. Elizabeth, Father Matthew Gottschalk of St. Francis, and Father Simeon Keogh of St. Benedict the Moor.

Monday morning, the day of the boycott, more than 500 children and parents showed up at St. Boniface to attend Freedom School. They found the doors closed. Father Groppi, however, met them outside and led them to the Metropolitan Baptist Church, about five blocks from St. Boniface.

Although the churches had closed their doors, neither Bishop Atkielski nor any other archdiocesan official had cleared up the matter of individual participation. There still was no specific mention of it in any communication from the bishop, and he continued to insist to reporters that the order did not ban individual participation. So Father Groppi and others made themselves useful.

Father Groppi, as might be expected, was the most noticeable. It was during this brief period that he began to emerge as one of Milwaukee's top civil rights leaders, and he did it with children — his favorite people. Children and teen-agers who were boycotting school flocked to Father Groppi as they had to no other leader in the boycott. It lasted a day and a half. On the afternoon of the second day of school boycott, Father Groppi received his walking papers from archdiocesan officials.

Under a direct order, Father Groppi obeyed. "We have disagreed, but we have obeyed," he said. It was the first and last time that the priest's superiors ever ordered him to stop his civil rights activities.

The reason for the order was not given, but it probably had something to do with the march Father Groppi led Monday night. Like so many other civil rights tactics, the march was a spur of the moment event. More that 200 young people went to St. Boniface Church for what was billed as an NAACP youth rally. By that time, Father Groppi, in addition to his membership in MUSIC, had been named state youth chairman for the NAACP. The group of young Negroes stayed only briefly at St. Boniface. Led by Father Groppi, they walked the few blocks to the boycott headquarters at St. Matthew's CME Church.

It was at this time that the priest first showed his uncanny ability to command the respect of black children. When the crowd of children marched into St. Matthew's Church, singing and chanting loudly, all it took to hush them completely was the sight of Father Groppi standing on a table with his hands raised.

There apparently had been no specific plans for a youth demonstration that night. In a speech at the St. Matthew rally, Barbee simply said: "Go to Director Foley's house and guarantee that he won't be able to fold up comfortably tonight." That was all the young people and Father Groppi needed. They left immediately and marched 38 blocks to Foley's home. About 50 persons who earlier had picketed the archdiocesan chancery office over the Freedom School business met them there.

It was at Foley's home that Father Groppi again demonstrated his Pied Piper control over the group of young people. The demonstrators were creating such a din with chants and songs as they marched in front of the house that a person had to shout in another's ear to converse.

Two police sergeants warned Father Groppi that he had to keep the marchers in single file. They also said he would have to quiet them down after 10 p.m. because of a city ordinance. By that time it already was past 10. "I can't promise to keep that group of young people in single file," Father Groppi said. "If you don't, Father, you're in trouble," one of the sergeants said.

One of them offered the priest the use of a loudspeaker attached to a squad car. Father Groppi climbed in the car, picked up the microphone, and spoke eight words: "This is Father Groppi. Can you hear me?"

It was as if the group of demonstrators had been struck dumb on the spot. Reporters who shouted to be heard inches away now could hear whispers from across the street. It was a display of discipline that the director of a military academy might have envied. And most of the young people on the picket line were not members of the privileged class. They were, for the most part, slum children.

"We have made our point," Father Groppi said over the loudspeaker. "Now we will march back to St. Boniface in prayerful silence." The demonstrators did just that. The only noise was an occasional murmur. They might have been a group of monks in a monastery for all the conversation that could be heard.

The march was the one that the mayor criticized when he accused boycott leaders of engaging in KKK tactics. Maier's criticisms apparently were based on erroneous information, because he said in his statement that the "bulk of the troops bent on bringing fear to John Foley's home are transients in the night, white students from other cities and other states who make their decisions about Milwaukee against their experiences at home." The fact of the matter was that almost all the marchers were Negro school pupils from Milwaukee.

Father Groppi was not the only priest barred from participation in the boycott. Father William Whelan, an assistant pastor at St. Gall's, another inner core church, was ordered to stop. But another priest — one as dedicated to the cause of civil rights as either of the others — found a way to teach in one of the Freedom Schools.

Father Patrick M. Flood, formerly an assistant pastor and one of the Milwaukee priests who went to Selma, was a student in the urban affairs department at the University of Wisconsin — Milwaukee at the time of the boycott. Teaching in a Freedom School, Father Flood explained, was part of a university assignment. It had to do with a seminar on social action. Father Flood called himself a "participating observer."

Pat, as most people he knew well called him, was a ruddy-faced, amiable young man with a ready laugh. Although he and Father Groppi were in almost total agreement on civil rights matters, Father Groppi was the sandpaper who rubbed the white majority raw, while Father Flood was the quicksilver whose best weapon was his charm. Pat Flood later would become the Milwaukee Archdiocese's first full-time specialist in urban affairs.

Following in the pattern of the one-day boycott in 1964, the three and one-half day boycott in October, 1965, was orderly and peaceful. There were no arrests for law violations related to it, although police did pick up truants daily and refer them to their parents. Policemen assigned to the nightly demonstrations — pickets went to the homes of Story and Vincent as well as Maier and Foley — volunteered the information that the demonstrators had behaved themselves very well.

No such statements were forthcoming in MUSIC's next civil rights campaign. About six weeks after the boycott, the committee started protesting the construction of a new elementary school in the inner core area.

The Edward A. McDowell Elementary School, public school officials said, would be the most modern school in the city. But to members of MUSIC, it was slated to be another Negro school and, as such, would be inferior. Beginning December 5, the civil rights organization conducted daily protests at the construction site of the new school. It is doubtful whether any of them actually believed they could halt construction. But they certainly made life difficult for the construction workers and police for 13 days.

The protest started with an all-night vigil at the school in below zero weather. As usual, Miss Morheuser was one of the demonstrators, her civil rights ardor unchilled by the biting wind.

The school construction site was surrounded by a six-foot high wire fence, with a gate at the north end. The gate fronted on an alley that divided the square block on which the school was being constructed. The area north of the alley was vacant land.

At 7:30 a.m. the morning of December 6, twenty-two civil rights demonstrators, including four clergymen — one of them was Father

Groppi — linked their arms together and formed a human chain in front of the gate. Some construction workers who arrived for work angrily shoved their way through the line. Several were Negroes. Police, fearing that a fight might break out, held other workers back until after the arrests.

Eleven of the 22, including Father Groppi and the other clergymen, were arrested when they refused to move away from the gate. It was Father Groppi's second, but not last, arrest in a civil rights cause. The other clergymen were Father Miles, Rev. Aukema, and Rev. David G. Owen, pastor of Wesley Methodist Church.

"This construction," MUSIC said in a statement, "is typical of northern style 'separate but equal' schools — schools well placed in neighborhoods which will obviously become racially imbalanced. Here the neighborhood school myth is unveiled for what it is meant to produce: Negro schools and white schools which operate outside the framework of democratic society. . . . Construction for segregation must stop. . . ."

MUSIC's tactics during the construction site demonstrations were based on an attempt to keep police off balance. Strategy varied from day to day. One day it was demonstrators trying to stop a truck from pouring concrete; the next, a youth chained himself to the construction site gate for more than four hours; on another occasion, marchers created a diversion by picketing at the gate while Miss Morheuser crawled through a hole in the fence with Ivy Morgan, a MUSIC member, and tried to help him chain himself to a fork lift. They were not fast enough and both were arrested.

The MacDowell demonstrations by MUSIC ended December 17. The following day, three civil rights organizations — MUSIC, the Marquette University Faculty Association for Interracial Justice, and the newly reorganized Milwaukee NAACP Youth Council — sponsored a march from the MacDowell school site to the school administration building 38 blocks away.

The march testified to the snowballing social awareness among priests, nuns, and other clergymen. Of about 285 persons in the march, more than one-third were Catholic priests and nuns, many of them from Marquette. Father Groppi was in the lead with Negro children. By now, Milwaukee newspapers were referring to him as "a leader in civil rights demonstrations."

The demonstration was the last of 1965. MUSIC already had announced that it planned selective boycotts of inner core schools during 1966. North Division, a high school that was 99 percent Negro, was selected as the first target. It became the only target. After postponements and delays, the North Division boycott finally came off March 28. Of the school's 1,548 students (eight of them white), 734 stayed away from school that day. This was about 500 more than the average number absent on any given day during the month.

After the North Division boycott, MUSIC slipped out of the militant civil rights scene in Milwaukee. The organization concentrated for a time on support of and opposition to various school board candidates, and it opposed a bond issue for school construction, contending that the bond issue would result in more segregated schools. But its major work came to be the tedious, detailed, preliminary investigations needed to prepare the case against the school board in the federal court suit. MUSIC's period of demonstrations and boycotts was over.

The Milwaukee United School Integration Committee never did win any victories, in the sense of budging the school board off the status quo. But it did manage to focus attention on the issue, and its position on de facto school segregation was largely vindicated. Two prestigious organizations studied the Milwaukee school system, and both told the school board, in effect, that it was responsible for the elimination of racial imbalance in the public schools.

One of the studies was the one recommended shortly before the school boycott of October, 1965. It was conducted by the Academy for Educational Development, a nonprofit educational research organization. We — Milwaukeeans, which recommended the study and paid half of its $114,500 cost, insisted that the boycott had nothing to do with its proposal. But it seems reasonably certain that the group would not have recommended the study had it not been for the continuing protest by MUSIC.

Similarly, Milwaukee was one of seven cities studied by the United States Commission on Civil Rights for its 1967 report, *Racial Isolation in the Public Schools.* Again, had it not been for the protests by MUSIC, Milwaukee might not have been chosen by the commission.

Civil rights leaders, who sneered at the We — Milwaukeeans study as another tactic for muzzling their protests, were vindicated in it. The study, released in September, 1967, almost parroted the points the civil rights organizations had been making since 1963. In the 400-page study, the sharpest criticism of the school board was leveled at its failure to recognize the existence of de facto school segregation.

"In relation to what other northern cities, large and small, are doing to reduce racial isolation, Milwaukee ranks rather low in terms of positive, constructive efforts being made by the school system, the board of school directors and citizen groups generally," the report said.

"Also," it added, "the Milwaukee public schools stand out by not having a public policy which acknowledges the inequity of racial isolation in the schools and the need for the schools to do something to eliminate it."

The Academy for Educational Development said there were three main reasons for reducing racial isolation in schools. For the similarity in reasoning, it might have been Barbee talking. The reasons given in the study were: the world, the country, and the city in which Milwaukee's children would live as adults would be multiracial; part of quality education is learning to understand and to work with persons of other races — as human beings, based on who and what they are rather than how they look or dress, and opportunities to work and play together would benefit white children as much as Negroes.

The school board's attitudes on the racial questions apparently made many school administrators and other personnel shy away from the issue. Academy researchers found that school personnel were reluctant to even discuss any evidence regarding adverse consequences of racial isolation. "There is even a hesitancy," the study said, "by school officers to research the situation. This is strange, knowing as they undoubtedly must that an understanding of the educational consequences of the mixing of students on racial grounds is of such importance in Milwaukee and throughout the nation."

Compensatory education, the school board's answer to the civil rights protests, also was roundly criticized in the study. The Academy researchers conceded that the list of compensatory education projects was impressive, but it found that the programs did not have the necessary air of emergency about them. The study also stated what the civil rights organizations had been saying all along, that some of the compensatory education programs smacked of tokenism because they dealt more with the general needs of masses of students than with the specialized needs of individual children.

There were other criticisms. But, most important, the study said in effect that neither racial integration nor compensatory education by themselves would solve problems in Milwaukee's inner core schools. What was needed, the Academy said, was a combination of the two. Again, this was what Barbee, Miss Morheuser, and other leaders in the Negro community had been saying all along.

The report of the United States Commission on Civil Rights, which focused only on the question of racial isolation in schools, was even more critical. It said that the Milwaukee school board, because of its policies and practices over the years, helped create a system of black and white schools, with the black schools winding up on the short end of the stick.

The school board, the commission said, had done little to bring Negro teachers and principals into the school system. Its policy of pupil transfers, in addition, had contributed to racial imbalance by permitting large numbers of white students to attend schools outside of Negro neighborhoods.

The commission's researchers also found that education was least effective in schools with large Negro enrollments, as shown by pupil achievement and ability tests. And, the commission's report added, the school board had chosen future school sites in locations that would insure maintenance of separate Negro and white schools.

"In Milwaukee," the report said, "the school people blame their own failures on disinterested parents and unmotivated children. This scapegoating device permits the Milwaukee school board and administration to feel no obligation to . . . seek new programs."

The report criticized the public school system's reliance on traditional programs for Negro students. "A program is no good if it does not work. The program of schooling does not work for the children in the predominantly Negro schools in Milwaukee." This being the case, the report said, school officials had the responsibility to find out why its programs were failing and to find alternatives.

School officials and board members, of course, denied most of the accusations in both reports. In the case of the report by the US Civil Rights Commission, they were able to fall back on their old tactic of attacking the people who prepared the report instead of discussing the report itself. Two of the Milwaukee consultants for the study were people with whom the board was quite familiar — Miss Morheuser and Harold Rose, a professor of geography at the University of Wisconsin — Milwaukee, who had been part of the parade of witnesses to appear before the school board's special committee to urge it to do something about the problem of de facto segregation.

Said Schools Superintendent Vincent: "On the basis of my impression of the people who prepared the report . . . I would expect it to be slanted against our schools. It would appear that several had predetermined conclusions in mind."

"He should attack the study," snapped one of the consultants, H. Millard Clements of the UW School of Education in Madison. "If he feels we were in error, he should point out specific errors in the study."

Ralph Schowalter, executive director of the Social Development Corp. in Washington, D. C., who conducted the Milwaukee study, said he alone had prepared it and none of those who had gathered the facts for it understood the overall picture.

School officials could not level similar charges against the We — Milwaukeeans study, because the committee that directed it was selected by the president of the school board, the schools superintendent, and We — Milwaukeeans. No one who could even remotely be considered a civil rights militant was on the committee.

At the end of 1967, the Milwaukee school board began its study of the study.

Civil rights organizations in Milwaukee and around the country have proven themselves prophetic many times since the modern civil rights movement first started prodding the American conscience in the mid-fifties. There is an essential justice in the cries of the civil rights advocates that makes fulfillment inevitable. It has not yet been otherwise. Complete fulfillment has not been reached in many areas, but the time will come. And when it comes, it will land on the side of the civil rights movement.

The Milwaukee United School Integration Committee won no victories while it was demonstrating. As with so many other civil rights organizations in other cities, it had to wait for history to judge the rightness of its protest.

VII

THE "WHITE NIGGER"

On August 14, 1967, nearly 1,000 persons, the majority of them white, gave three lengthy standing ovations to James Edward Groppi, Catholic priest, adviser to the Milwaukee NAACP Youth Council and the city's number 1 civil rights figure.

A little over two weeks later, more than 1,000 persons, all of them white, screamed obscenities and hurled bottles, stones, and chunks of concrete at the same man as he marched on the south side of Milwaukee with a group of Negroes and whites who wanted the city to pass an open housing ordinance.

The standing ovations came at a testimonial dinner for Father Groppi in the sparkling student union of the University of Wisconsin — Milwaukee. Sixteen speakers gave testimonial speeches in his honor. His mother, five sisters, and four brothers were among the guests. One of the speakers, the Rev. Lucius Walker, another civil rights leader and a black man, told the dinner guests that they were having a unique historical experience.

"It isn't often you see a saint in the flesh," he said, "and I literally consider Jim one of the saints of the church."

The rocks, bottles and obscenities came during the second march to the south side by the youth council, August 29. There, at a used car lot along the line of march, a grotesque effigy of Father Groppi swung by its neck from a light pole. Young men waved signs saying, "Groppi — Black God" and "Trained Nigger."

There was little ambivalence in Milwaukee toward Father Groppi in late 1967. Mere mention of the name was certain to produce a reaction from any Milwaukeean. Reactions varied, but usually they were of the extreme kind — extremely in favor of the priest or extremely against him. There were, however, a few who were circumspect about the priest and the young Negroes of his youth council and his commando force. They believed that Father Groppi, if nothing else, was a valuable safety valve, providing an outlet through which Milwaukee's alienated Negroes could vent their frustrations.

But most of the reaction to Father Groppi was of the unprintable kind. One of the epithets heard most often — that was printable — was "white nigger." To Father Groppi, of course, such an epithet was a compliment, for he had accomplished what few white men have ever been able to do — think like an American Negro. He would deny it, saying that no white man could know what it was like to be a black man. But the black men around him knew that he knew what it was like, because he had lived it. It had even crept, unconsciously, into his speech patterns. When Father Groppi spoke about black people — he did not like the word Negro — the pronoun used was always "we," not "they." Even so, the priest was constantly aware of the fact that he was a white man. He often said that any white person in the civil rights movement, himself included, had to constantly re-evaluate his own position and his own motives.

Father Groppi ascended to his position as Milwaukee's leading civil rights militant, and a national civil rights figure as well, in the short space of two and one-half years. He did it with irreverence, nerve, dedication, and a disorganized kind of determination that kept people, even those close to him, wondering what he was going to do next.

The irreverence was for anything and anybody official whom Father Groppi believed was not doing enough about the problems of black people. This could, and did, include anybody from the archbishop to the mayor to the governor. The nerve and dedication were those of the true believer — Father Groppi was willing to take almost any chance to further the cause. He was, and is, disorganized in the sense that he lives for the moment, disdains the past, and plans little for the future.

He also was a frequent and outspoken critic of his own church, a fact that made his *persona non grata* with many Milwaukee area priests, some of whom attacked him and his methods from their pulpits. Father Groppi had been fortunate in having as his pastor Father Eugene F. Bleidorn, a quiet, compassionate man with a deep understanding of the problems of Milwaukee's ghetto. He backed Father Groppi to the utmost and, if he ever disagreed with the fiery young priest, he never made it known publicly.

Father Bleidorn left St. Boniface in late summer, 1967, because of illness. Archbishop Cousins then converted the operation of the parish into the first team pastorate in the city, with Father Groppi and three other young priests running the parish on an equal and cooperative basis. Father Michael Neuberger, who had been serving as an assistant with Father Groppi, became the administrator for the parish. Father Neuberger was another young priest, like Father Flood, who had a deep commitment to the cause of civil rights and the problems of Milwaukee's inner core, but he worked quietly in the background and seldom appeared in public demonstrations. He proved himself to be an effective speaker before white audiences, however.

Although Father Groppi was in a situation in which he could operate with relative freedom, he still yearned for a parish of his own that he could operate independently. In late 1967, he said he wanted a church that would function as more than just a place of worship, a church that would have kitchen facilities where the poor could get meals, and a place that could serve as a haven for people with no other place to stay. "If I needed the room," he said, "I could take out the pews in the church and put up some beds."

Such a church, Father Groppi believed, would bring in people from the community. The church would have a "meaningful liturgy," of the sort Father Groppi developed with members of the youth council. He often offered Mass in his suit — no vestments — and the young people would gather around the altar. They sang black spirituals and discussed events of the day that affected them.

On one such occasion, October 13, 1967, a commando and about a dozen young girls who were members of the youth council gathered around the St. Boniface altar to celebrate Mass with Father Groppi. They sang "Mary Had a Baby," "Nobody Knows the Trouble I've Seen," and "Swing Low, Sweet Chariot" during the Mass. After the Communion of the Mass, the following exchange took place (Father

Groppi's comments are indicated by "G" and the response from the young people by "A"):

G: Ever hear of James Baldwin? He's a black author. He was raised in the slums of Harlem, just a high school graduate, one of the best authors in the country today. And he writes about the slums. Very militant, angry young man. One of the things James Baldwin says is this: Says there's some white people I like and some white people I don't like. Some black people I like and some black people I don't like. Think that's true?

A: Uh-huh.

G: You like all black people?

A: Unh-uh.

G: You like all white people?

A: Unh-uh.

G: What do we mean when we sing that song, "Hear me I'm calling, my brothers"?

A: It means we want to be heard all over.

G: What did Dick Gregory mean when he went down to jail and the police officer asked him, he said, "You got any brothers and sisters?" "Yeah," he says, "you take all the people in the world and subtract myself, they're all my brothers and sisters." What'd he mean by that?

A: Everybody in the world is his brother and sister.

G: All right, so that's what we talk about and that's what we sing about.

After the Mass was over, the young people started chanting, "Black power's coming, black power." Father Groppi interrupted.

G: What do we mean by black power? Does it mean black people over white people?

A: No, equal! It means opportunity.

G: All right. Do black people have much money?

A: No.

G: Then what do we call it, what kind of power do we call it? . . . Money power, economic power.

A: And in the political field, and in the social . . .

G: Political power. What do we mean by political power?

A: In the political field, we want some black people in office and not just white people.

G: What do we mean by educational power?

A: We want to get a good education.

G: What's one aspect of our education we don't get?

A: Negro history.

G: Black history — all right.

A: And a secondary education.

G: Black history — good.

The young people — most of them in the sixth, seventh, and eighth grades — chanted again, "Move over whitey, black power." Then they ended their participation in the Mass by singing, "We love everybody in our hearts."

It is this sort of liturgy that Father Groppi believes is meaningful to people in the black community. "We enjoy ourselves there," he says. "We can offer Mass with the emphasis on this being the source of strength for us to go out into the community and to feed the poor and clothe the naked, to get involved in social action."

He has little patience with the trappings and rituals of his church. "Vigil lights, definitely all this sort of nonsense has to go," he once said. "These ecclesiastical gymnastics. I think the vestments have to go, too. They're the ordinary garb of people 2,000 years ago. My God, I don't know what in the world we're doing wearing the garb that people wore 2,000 years ago. To some people these have meaning — a great deal of meaning — but to most of the young people whom I associate with, they look at this garb that the priest's got on, and they laugh. It's so out of this world; it's so outlandish. . . .

"These ecclesiastical gymnastics are much of what is present in our churches today. . . . A person performed these actions and this in itself is holiness. It isn't. These are means to an end; the end is social involvement, a change in the community, the alleviation of suffering humanity. As long as prayer and the Mass and everything else is aimed toward this, how this is going to have a meaningful change in my life, and in the lives of suffering people in the community, well then I believe it's relevant. But if you're just going to do this as an end in itself — well then, I don't want to have any part of it. . . .

"We talk about the sufferings of black people and the injustices of society, the meaning behind black spirituals. The kids listen and they're reverent. When we start praying for individuals who have been arrested or have been beaten by the police, they listen, and the Mass suddenly has meaning for them."

Father Groppi is soft spoken in private conversation. But in civil rights rallies he has often shouted in anger, his voice cracking. He believes clergymen have to stop preaching "pie in the sky" to oppressed black people. And he is an advocate of black power and self-determination for Negroes. "The Lord ain't gonna help you, and he ain't gonna help me unless we get out and help ourselves," he said at rallies in St. Boniface Church. "Jesus Christ was a civil rights worker. The greatest civil rights worker, greater than anyone here. No one here has ever been nailed to a cross."

And again: "You must involve yourself as Christ did. The peace of Jesus Christ was the peace of inner conviction. He preached the peace of human dignity. He never meant that creative tension should be removed from the earth. He didn't say that he came to bring peace to the earth — that's part of the white lie — but rather to cast a sword upon the earth. You must be revolutionaries. Christ was a revolutionary. That's why he ended up on a cross."

The Pharisees of modern times, Father Groppi believes, are public officials and "a lot of priests and ministers who walk the streets and don't do a damn thing about the black man being treated second rate."

Father Groppi has rarely put anything in writing, preferring to expound his beliefs in speeches. But on one occasion, in November, 1967, he fired off an angry letter to the pastor of a church in the southwestern Milwaukee suburb of West Allis. The pastor, Msgr. Oscar Winninghoff of St. Aloysius Church, had cited an example from St. Boniface Church in a parish bulletin item on admonishing sinners. He said that a few years before, a former pastor at St. Boniface had told him that there were four boys in the parish who had the same mother but all had different fathers.

The situation posed a problem for the pastor, Msgr. Winninghoff wrote. He could not simply tell the boys, "Your mother is no good."

"Perhaps," he wrote, "you could go to the mother and say: 'It is praiseworthy to have children but Jesus instituted the Sacrament of Matrimony so that a couple might have God's blessing and bring babies into the world. Matrimony also gives couples the grace to rear their children. God also said a man should have one wife and a wife should have one husband.' "

Then, speaking of the four boys and how to handle them, the monsignor said: "Would integration solve the problem? If we would take these four boys into St. Aloysius school could we imbue them with the ideal of a holy marriage and of Catholic family life? If we would exchange four of our boys and send them into St. Boniface

School would they maintain the ideal of Catholic family life and of Catholic marriage? It is easy to go downhill but hard to go uphill. Which families from St. Aloysius would volunteer to send their boys into St. Boniface School as exchange students? Who would pay the transportation, etc.? We would end up in a regrettable situation. How would we remedy this situation? A priest, interested enough, might with the help of God, solve the problem, if he could call into play all the spiritual works of mercy; to instruct the ignorant, to counsel the doubtful, and to admonish the sinner."

Father Groppi's reply showed his view of Christianity and Catholicism, and their relation to people. He wrote:

Dear Rev. Winninghoff:

Your parish bulletin of November 12th has reached the desks of the priests at St. Boniface. Some of your concerned parishioners were deeply scandalized and sent the bulletins here. I cannot understand how a man who proclaims to be a follower of Jesus Christ could write such racist trash. Christ worked with the poor, the Samaritan, the Publican, the sinner, the afflicted, and all others who were socially ostracized. He understood their problems and He had empathy for their sufferings. He was crucified for His associations, and His defense of the unacceptable. He admonished the Samaritan woman at the well. He did not call her "no good." He certainly did not implicate in any way that the nature of the woman's weakness had anything to do with the fact that she was a Samaritan. He never said that the Samaritan had to rise to a new height of morality before he could enjoy the right of freedom of association. In fact, Christ preferred the morality of the poor, and those relegated to secondary status in society by reason of ethnic origin. It was the hypocrisy of the Scribes and Pharisees that bothered Him. Christ's attitude towards the Pharisaism in your bulletin was expressed in the words "whitened sepulchre." John the Baptist used stronger words, "offspring of vipers."

Your problem, Father Winninghoff, is a common problem in white society. You want black people to be as moral as you would like to be. I do not deny that there are weaknesses in the black family structure. But then it has been a racist attitude such as yours that has destroyed it. Perhaps you ought to read a little history. I do not want to get into a lengthy discussion on black family life. I agree with William Stringfellow that it is wrong to talk about the weaknesses of the black family structure without talking about its inherent strengths and beauty. And that it is wrong to talk about the emasculation of the black male without talking about the defeminization of the white female. I will never tell the black people in this parish to pattern their lives after a supposedly more moral white society. By example, you have nothing to offer us but racism and oppression. The conduct of white society in this country has hardly been Christian. This is particularly understandable when men who assume the role of Christian leadership such as yourself distort the teachings of the Jew of Nazareth, as you did in last Sunday's bulletin.

I was disturbed that you did not mention the name of the pastor who made the remark about the woman with the four children. You may have implicated the wrong man, and, therefore, ruined the reputation of a true follower of Jesus Christ. I know that it was not Father Bleidorn. I worked with him for two years and I know that his understanding of poverty is Christ-like. He does not waste time sipping martinis and gossiping about the personal problems of his parishioners in priestly circles. I imagine all the priests in that circle had a good laugh about the woman with four sons and no husband. Laugh yourselves into hell. I know that in the eyes of God she is more beautiful than every priest in that sewing circle. You see, her problem is circumstantial, but yours is hypocrisy. She is the victim of a sick and racist society. Your sin is pride. The pastor who made that remark proved something. He proved what I have been saying for a long time, and that is that few white priests, sisters, teachers, policemen have understanding and empathy of what it means to be black in white America. And that unless a man realizes that it is a privilege to live and work in the black community, he ought to get out. We don't need him and we don't want him.

Christ failed in his efforts to make the Pharisees understand. He did try. I suppose that this is partially why I am taking time to write to you. However, I am more concerned about the people, black and white, who read that scandalous nonsense. Let me try to explain by giving you an example of how some people suffer from American racism.

About 12 years ago, I met a woman living in unbelievable poverty. She was living in the vicinity of St. Joseph's parish. The church is gone now, the expressway, you know. It was rebuilt in an affluent white neighborhood. There are more Catholics there of course, and this is where our work lies, doesn't it, Msgr. Winninghoff? I know that you will not agree with this, but that church should have been replaced immediately. Christ's primary concern was for the poor and the ostracized. When will men like you learn that? Anyway this woman had five children. She came from Mississippi. She never learned how to read and write because the white man in the south told her that she had no time for that. All her life she was called a nigger, and that the purpose of her life was to pick the white man's cotton and satisfy his lust. She came to Milwaukee looking for a better life, but did not find it. The people in your parish do not know hunger, do they, Father Winninghoff? She and her children knew what it was like to be hungry and to live in a rat-infested shack. You see, she could not get any welfare money because she was not in Milwaukee for a year. And what employer is going to hire a black woman from Mississippi who cannot read or write. She found a job, finally, picking chicken feathers for less than 50c an hour. She got tired of begging and seeing her children hungry. Yes, you guessed it; she became a so-called prostitute. She sold her body evenings so that her children could eat the next day. It is a tragedy that Pharisees like yourself can judge so easily and shout — "adultress." It reminds me of a scene from the gospel. Recall for a moment that scene of the weeping woman at the feet of Jesus, and listen again to His words, "Let him who is without sin among you cast the first stone." You, Father Winninghoff, have had the audacity to throw the first stone.

Father Groppi was not a man to mince words. His tone was sometimes threatening. He told an audience in Chicago that he had heard of an incident in which a 12-year-old girl was thrown to the ground and kicked in the stomach by a policeman. "If that ever happens in my presence and I have a baseball bat in my hand," he said, "someone is going to get his head bashed in."

He also shocked Milwaukeeans, along with audiences in other cities — including people watching television in Kansas City one time — by saying that a policeman who had arrested him called him a "fucking white nigger." Although in private he sometimes talked in the language of the streets, he did not use that particular four-letter word except in quoting the policeman. He said he used the quote in speeches to show the sort of racism that black people faced in the ghetto. Nonetheless, his use of the quote fueled the hatred toward him among many white Milwaukeeans.

James Groppi was born November 16, 1930, in a south side area of Milwaukee near Lake Michigan known as Bay View. His parents, Giocondo and Giorgina Groppi, had twelve children, of which James was the eleventh. Two of them died before Jim was born.

Giocondo Groppi was an immigrant Italian who had come to Milwaukee in 1913. He operated a grocery store in the Italian neighborhood in which the family lived. Jim and his brothers and sisters all worked in the store. His father died in 1956 while Father Groppi was in the seminary, but other members of the family still operate the store.

James Groppi's childhood was not unlike that of many other Catholic boys in Milwaukee. He attended a parochial grade school (Immaculate Conception), where the nuns hammered knowledge into the students. In those days, most Catholic schools were tougher on a student than most public schools. This was one reason why Father Groppi said he had a "four year vacation in high school."

He attended Bay View High School, one of the schools in the Milwaukee public school system. Jim Groppi had a strong interest in athletics — football, baseball, and basketball in grade school and basketball in high school. He played first string guard his last two years at Bay View, and was captain of the team during his senior year.

If he had any influence in his early years that might point toward his later work with black people in Milwaukee's ghetto, Father Groppi would probably say it was his father. Giocondo Groppi spoke broken English and sometimes suffered what Father Groppi calls "humorous contempt." To this day, the priest cannot stand nationality jokes, particularly "nigger jokes."

When Father Groppi was growing up, Italians in Milwaukee were a minority group. Immaculate Conception Church, Father Groppi contends, was an Irish parish, and Italians were not made to feel welcome there. He remembers when an Italian priest used to celebrate Mass for Bay View Italians in a shoemaker's shop. None of the Groppi children, he recalled, was baptized at Immaculate Conception. They were taken down to Blessed Virgin of Pompeii Church in the Italian third ward of Milwaukee for baptism.

But in spite of the prejudice sometimes directed at him, Giocondo Groppi did not permit himself or his family to retaliate in kind. Words like "nigger," "polak," "mick," or any other derogatory nationality epithet were not permitted in the Groppi household. It was like calling an Italian a "dago" or a "wop," Giocondo told his children.

Even though Father Groppi experienced what it was like to be a member of a minority group, he disdains comparisons between his experience and that of a Negro in modern American society. When his father arrived in Milwaukee around 1913, Father Groppi said, "the Italian was in pretty bad shape. But nothing as far as the black man is concerned. I don't like these comparisons between various ethnic groups and the black man because there are so many differences. Just the black man's color was enough."

Although there are some similarities between his background and that of the young Negroes with whom he works, Father Groppi does not like to talk about it. "There are so damn many differences," he says. "An Italian is white, and that's everything. . . . Being raised in an Italian community does not make a man understand what another ethnic group such as the black man in this country goes through. You can get some similarities. For example, the Jewish people. You'll get some Jewish people who really have a great deal of empathy because many of the people who have escaped, for example, the concentration camps in Germany have come here and they look at the black man and they have a greater understanding. Yet you've got others that step on people below them for the purpose of acceptance. Now this is true with Italians. Some of the worst bigots in this country are Italians who have gone through terrific suffering in the past. And yet they'll turn around and step on black people."

Father Groppi's first experience with a black man was on the basketball court. It happened during a game between Bay View High School and Lincoln High School, which had a few Negro players. One of them was driving in for a shot, and Jim Groppi, knowing he could not block the shot, hit his opponent with a body block that flipped him over and sent him sliding across the floor into the crowd. Jim went over and offered to help the player up, but got a kick in the stomach for his trouble.

Later, after the game, the two young men apologized to each other — Groppi for throwing the block, the young Negro for kicking him in the gut. They shook hands and smiled. Groppi later wrote a high school English theme on brotherhood and racial justice and used the incident to illustrate how he had learned something about the subject firsthand.

After high school, young Groppi continued to play basketball. He earned money by setting pins at a bowling alley that, some 18 years later, he would walk past in an open housing march on Milwaukee's south side. A year after his graduation from high school, he entered Mount Calvary Seminary in Fond du Lac, Wisconsin.

Why the seminary? "I didn't see anything around," he said. "To me, life, in order to have meaning, had to have religion. The brevity of life is one thing that always hit me — the shortness. You're here today and you're gone the next day. You've got to do something in this short expanse of time in order to make eternity meaningful."

It was during his seminary years that Father Groppi began developing an empathy with the black poor. He worked summers at a youth center in Milwaukee's inner core. It was there that he saw the social suffering and ostracism that Negroes lived with every day.

He also observed prejudice in the seminary. "There were instances of prejudice that were horrible, really horrible," he once said. "Nigger talk. Nigger jokes." One year his class at St. Francis Seminary (he studied there after finishing at Mount Calvary) put on a minstrel show. "I refused to attend," he said. "They could not see that this was insulting to the black community. They could not see that here again the Negro was being portrayed as a poor, meek, docile, musical creature."

After ordination, Father Groppi was assigned to a white parish on Milwaukee's south side. Some of his parishioners there later welcomed him back to the south side by marching with him and the Milwaukee NAACP Youth Council during the violent open housing demonstrations of late summer 1967.

In 1963, Father Groppi was assigned to St. Boniface, once an all-German parish but by then a church in a neighborhood that was almost all Negro. His early civil rights activities brought no headlines. During his summer vacations he drove to Mississippi with young Milwaukee Negroes to participate in civil rights activities that included integrating restaurants and helping Negroes register to vote.

But it was not until March, 1965, that public attention in Milwaukee became focused on Father Groppi. Even then, he was only one of a group of priests and nuns in Selma, Alabama. That was when I first met him. My initial impression was of a restless and serious young man, preoccupied with the moment, always looking over his shoulder to see if something was happening that he might be missing. His preoccupation with the events going on around him made him seem cold, the sort of person who would be difficult to get to know. But then, I was a newspaperman, and Father Groppi had little interest in publicity.

He was much more interested in the black children who populated the shacks on the dirt streets in the Negro sections of Selma. Civil rights leaders had instructed priests, nuns, and other clergy and religious in Selma to stick together in groups when they ventured outside the George Washington Carver Housing Project — center of the civil rights demonstrations. The reason was fear that some of them might be attacked by "rednecks" or Ku Klux Klansmen. They also were instructed never to walk more than two abreast because they might be arrested for staging a parade.

It was about a mile from the housing project to St. Elizabeth's, a Negro mission church. Every morning, the four Catholic priests from Milwaukee — Fathers Groppi, Flood, Schlaefer, and Gottschalk — walked from the housing project where they were staying with Negro families to the church for Mass.

They stuck together, too — except for Father Groppi. One minute he would be there, the next minute he would be gone — down a dusty side street, heedless of his own safety, to sit on a rickety porch or in the dust of a grassless yard to play with the little black children. Few shied away from him. The other priests had little choice but to wait for him or go back and round him up. But a block later he would be gone again.

There was an impatience and an impulsiveness about Father Groppi that showed there in Selma. Around noon on March 16, 1965, a quiet day in Selma, word arrived via the civil rights grapevine that possemen on horseback in Montgomery, 50 miles away, had charged into a line of demonstrators from the Student Nonviolent Co-ordinating Committee (SNCC), clubbing and injuring some of them.

Hardly had the news began circulating than Father Groppi was ready to go, his suitcase in his car. The three other Milwaukee priests, who had traveled to Selma in Father Groppi's Dodge, had to run and get their suitcases while he sat impatiently in the car with the motor running. Two clergymen from Worcester, Massachusetts, decided to go along — Father Donald Gonynor, a hip young priest, and the Rev. Jan Selby, a tall, quiet, Methodist minister — but they left their clothes behind because Father Groppi was in such a sweat to get going.

His haste almost got the lot of them in trouble. Just outside the city limits of Selma, Father Groppi gunned the Dodge hard. Almost immediately, he had an Alabama state police car on his tail, riding the bumper. Father Groppi slowed quickly, too soon for the state policeman to clock him for speeding. The police car hung on the bumper of Father Groppi's car for several miles, hoping, I supposed, to rattle him. I was following behind in a rented car with Bob Leipzig of the *Milwaukee Sentinel,* who had ridden to Selma with the four Milwaukee priests.

The state policeman soon tired of baiting Father Groppi. He swung out and shot past. As soon as he was out of sight, Father Groppi speeded up, this time carefully watching, as I was, for other police cruisers.

No one, least of all Father Groppi, knew exactly what he would do when he got to Montgomery. All Father Groppi knew was that some young civil rights workers had been hurt and he was going to help in whatever way he could. He, most of all, would have done anything asked of him.

By asking directions in Montgomery's Negro area, where many

small groups of Negro and white civil rights workers stood talking quietly, the clergymen finally found a small white frame house at the corner of Bolivar and Dericote streets. The Rev. Martin Luther King, Jr., they were told, was inside conferring with James Forman, then the head of SNCC. Mr. King would tell them what to do.

It was more than four hours before they found out anything. And even then, the only information was that Mr. King would speak at a rally at the nearby Beulah Baptist Church that evening. The priests headed there immediately, except for Father Schlaefer, who became ill and went to St. John the Baptist Church, a Catholic mission in the heart of the black ghetto of Montgomery.

No one who attended that rally could ever forget it. A San Francisco newsman told me that the last time he had heard such a din was at a Beatles performance. Most of those in the church were Negro teen-agers and college students. It was so packed that some people literally were hanging from the rafters. I was perched high on a narrow window sill. Hundreds of others crowded outside around windows and the doors.

When the clergymen arrived, they were ushered to the front, to several pews at the side. A husky young Negro in coveralls led songs and cheers, and the Milwaukee priests, particularly Father Groppi, joined in enthusiastically.

When Mr. King walked into the sanctuary from a door behind the altar, an hour late as usual, the roar of the crowd in the church almost lifted the roof off. It was like standing near the exhaust of a jet airliner.

It took nearly two hours for all the speeches — by Mr. King; James Forman, who shocked the assemblage by inadvertently blurting out a four-letter obscenity, and the Rev. Ralph D. Abernathy, King's top aide, who smoothed things over quickly. Then Abernathy asked the clergymen in the church to march to the Alabama capitol and conduct a prayer vigil there.

It was seven-tenths of a mile from the church to the beautiful white capitol building of the state of Alabama. Father Groppi and the Milwaukee priests were near the front of the line.

There were 35 clergymen in the march, and when they arrived at the front steps of the capitol, they found themselves outnumbered more than 2 to 1 by Alabama state policemen. The situation soon became a battle of nerves. The clergymen wanted to walk up the steps to say a prayer. The major in charge of the state policemen said they had to stay on the sidewalk, and he had a solid line of state troopers to back him up.

Father Daniel Mallette of Chicago, who acted as the spokesman for the group, said the clergymen would not leave until they could have their prayer on the steps. They knelt down. Father Mallette read from St. Paul's Epistle to the Hebrews. Father Groppi knelt with his arms folded. When Father Mallette asked for discussion of the Epistle, Father Groppi was the first to speak.

"God is the Father of us all," he said, "and we are all brothers in him. We have an obligation to help our brothers. . . . If we go to church on Sunday and preach the doctrine of Christ and then do nothing . . . we are hypocrites."

Finally, the major in charge of the state policemen relented and permitted the clergymen to mount the stairs for their prayer. Although most of them were Catholic priests, they recited the Protestant version of the Lord's Prayer — it was longer than the Catholic version, they said.

Later, on the way back, Father Groppi commented: "That's something I've always wanted to do — sit down in the heart of the segregationist south with a group of priests and ministers in an ecumenical protest."

"You just have a martyr complex is all," Father Gottschalk kidded him.

The following day, the Milwaukee priests, along with the Rev. Richard Aukema, marched on the Dallas county courthouse in Montgomery and stood in the rain for more than three hours while Mr. King conferred with city and county officials. It was to be their last demonstration in Alabama. After spending the night at St. John the Baptist Church, the priests drove Rev. Aukema back to Selma, then returned to Milwaukee.

But Father Groppi brought with him some of the fervor of those Alabama demonstrations. Most clergymen who were there agreed that the entire situation had about it the aspects of an intense religious retreat. The atmosphere reeked of brotherhood and rightness. Those who were there had a feeling that what they were doing was so right that they had to prevail, had to overcome.

A popular topic of conversation in Selma and Montgomery was: "Why Selma? And why Montgomery? Why not in your own back yard? What are we doing here when there are problems back home?"

The answer for many — not only clergymen — was that Alabama offered rewards. The rewards were not the usual sort. A reward might be getting hit over the head with a club by a posseman, or getting one's self arrested in the cause. You could get this in Alabama, where the issues were sharply defined. It was something tangible, whereas at home you might work with black people and on the problems of black people for years and no one would ever respond one way or the other. The reward up north was apathy — like beating your head against a wall of gelatin. There was a harder wall in the south.

Whether these were Father Groppi's thoughts at the time, I do not know. It is apparent, however, that he was not the sort to quietly become exasperated beating his head against a wall of apathy. He would create resistance and then agitate against it for all he was worth.

Father Groppi's involvement in the civil rights struggle started in Milwaukee with the Milwaukee United School Integration Committee. He shocked a lot of people, particularly when he was arrested for blocking a school bus and, later, for blocking the gate to the construction site of the MacDowell School. Requests started coming into the Milwaukee chancery office asking Archbishop William E. Cousins to either muzzle or transfer the young priest. It is to the archbishop's credit that he had the foresight not to take such action. Had he removed Father Groppi, he would have removed that "safety valve" for which some Milwaukeeans have been thankful.

The incident during the school boycott with Bishop Atkielski was the only time Father Groppi ever was ordered to stop any civil rights activity in Milwaukee. It is doubtful that the action would have been taken had the archbishop not been away at the time, first attending the Vatican Council in Rome and later on a pilgrimage through the Holy Land. On his return, the archbishop hedged somewhat on questions about Father Groppi, saying he did not always think the young priest prudent. But the archbishop was wise enough to know that he was not close enough to Father Groppi's situation to know all about it. He said he thought, for one thing, that Father Groppi had "a lot of guts."

At the time, Father Groppi scandalized churchgoers who held to the traditional belief that priests belonged in pulpits on Sunday and nuns ought to stay in convents. But as yet there was little violent reaction against the priest. That had to wait until after Wauwatosa.

Shortly after the school boycott of 1965, a group of young Negroes — members of the Milwaukee NAACP Youth Council — asked Father Groppi to be their adviser. The youth council had been around a long time — since 1947 — but, like the adult branch of the NAACP in Milwaukee, it had never been a particularly militant organization.

Because it was a youth group — there was no minimum age limit — it had always had advisers. John Givens, chairman of the Milwaukee CORE chapter during the demonstrations against the Social Development Commission, had once been an adviser to the youth council.

Father Groppi was a logical choice for the newly reorganized youth council. At the time, he was the NAACP's state youth chairman.

By early summer, 1966, the youth council and Father Groppi had their first big civil rights issue. It was an issue that was to put the national spotlight on Milwaukee again — it seemed that every time Father Groppi became involved in a civil rights campaign, it was national news. This probably was because he was a white priest who was acting like a militant young Negro. But he also was helped along to national prominence by none other than Milwaukee's Mayor Henry W. Maier.

VIII

EAGLES AND OPEN HOUSING

Early in 1966, the Milwaukee NAACP Youth Council started its first big civil rights campaign. It involved an issue that was widely misunderstood, but even when understood, it was perhaps the least popular civil rights issue ever to arise in the country.

The youth council decided to protest the membership of public officials in the Fraternal Order of Eagles, a nation-wide club that restricted its membership to Caucasians. To understand the issue, one has to understand the Milwaukee Aerie of the Eagles club. With 5,400 members, it was the second largest Eagles club in the nation.

In Milwaukee, membership in the Eagles club was almost a political necessity. Club members consisted of every class of white people, from factory workers to labor leaders and professional people — the kind of people any politician needed communication with. Most members of the city's political power structure also belonged.

Among the members in 1966 were 17 circuit and county judges, 10 of 24 county supervisors, the district attorney, county treasurer, circuit court clerk, 10 of 19 city aldermen, the city attorney, city treasurer, city comptroller, city clerk, and the executive secretary of the city election commission.

Wisconsin's fourth district congressman, Clement Zablocki, who represented Milwaukee's south side, was an Eagle, and Governor

Warren P. Knowles held an honorary membership in the club. Henry S. Reuss, the fifth district congressman whose territory included most of the area in which Milwaukee's Negroes lived, had been a member but resigned almost as soon as the issue was raised. Four top county officials also had been members, but had let their memberships lapse or had resigned before the youth council started protesting. They were the county executive, the sheriff, the county treasurer, and the register of deeds.

To the young men and women of the youth council, the restrictive membership policy was irritating enough in itself — another door in the community that was closed to Negroes. But the fact that so many public officials, particularly judges, belonged to the club, was even more salt in the wound. Father Groppi told a group of white clergymen that he could not understand how judges could belong to a segregated club and then sit in judgment on men of all races. "Could you sit in front of a man with a black face who belonged to the Black Muslims?" he asked.

The answer, of course, would be no. Black Muslims are antiwhite. In American society, that means they are extremists. If a white man is anti-Negro, he is merely an average citizen.

The youth council's protest actually started out against the restrictive membership policy. For several weeks in February and March of 1966, youth council members picketed the Eagles club building. But they attracted almost no attention. Television and the daily press virtually ignored the young demonstrators, perhaps because of the issue involved. Even some civil rights liberals, at the outset, thought the youth council's protest was a bit silly. Private clubs, they said, had a right to set whatever membership policies they pleased.

This was where some of the misunderstanding came in. Although the youth council was protesting the membership policy — mostly on the basis that the club was more public than private — its main point was that public officials, whose duty it was to serve all groups of people, should not belong to a segregated club. Such membership by a public official, the youth council argued, was morally wrong.

The situation did produce a dilemna. Youth council members were exercising their constitutional rights of speech and assembly to protest the rights of certain individuals to freely associate with persons of their choosing. There was little question of the right, from a legal and constitutional standpoint, of the judges and public officials to belong to the club. But it did seem to be, at least, inconsistent. Many of them said they deplored the whites-only policy. But they would not quit, saying they preferred to work for reform from within the club.

The Eagles argued the issue mostly from the standpoint of a man's right to belong to a club and the club's right to set its membership requirements. There was little discussion of the issue of a public official's or judge's membership. Club membership, the Eagles said, was an aspect of private life and had nothing to do with public life.

The youth council's protest was interrupted in early August by the blast of a bomb that tore apart the office of the Milwaukee branch of the NAACP. The explosion blew out windows, knocked plaster off the walls, flattened doors in the office, and started a series of small fires. Firemen were able to extinguish them with hand pumps. Fortunately, no one was in the offices at the time. Two families lived in apartments over the offices, but the explosion did not reach them.

Two Milwaukee men who were identified as members of the Ku Klux Klan later were arrested and charged with damaging property with explosives. The charge against one of them was dismissed and the other — Robert C. Schmidt — pleaded guilty and was convicted of the charge.

Father Groppi earlier had established a Freedom House for the youth council. It was a dilapidated old slum dwelling on North Fifth Street in one of Milwaukee's worst neighborhoods. The purpose of the house was to bring Father Groppi and the youth council members in closer contact with poor people in the neighborhood, particularly young people. The house also served as a home for Father Groppi, some of the commandos and youth council members, and others who had nowhere else to go. Later the house was condemned. Father Groppi moved back to St. Boniface and the youth council rented another old house on Fifteenth Street in a rundown area slated for urban renewal. The Fifteenth Street house later was fire bombed and became a rallying point in the youth council's 1967 open housing marches.

Two days after the August 9, 1966, bombing of the NAACP office, several young men who were members of the youth council started guarding the Fifth Street Freedom House with a loaded carbine. The gun was Father Groppi's idea. He said that there had been threatening calls to the St. Boniface rectory following the bombing. The callers, he said, had told him he was next.

Milwaukee's white majority diverted its attention from the bombing and focused on the potential victims. The fact that a group of young Negroes publicly announced that they were defending their Freedom House from a possible attack became a source of irritation and concern for many Milwaukeeans. There were rumors that Archbishop Cousins had been asked to take action against the priest. It was an old story all over again. No one would have gotten upset over any white person who kept a loaded gun to defend his home against an imagined attack from Negroes.

The archbishop, however, said there had been no petitions. "Unquestionably, there are those who are not in sympathy with all of his actions," he said, referring to Father Groppi. "This is to be expected. I think that in some instances there would be a matter of judgment or of timing, but I feel that a man assigned to a specific work should be allowed to work in that field. I think that his action comes in the area of city ordinance. If he is violating an ordinance, then I think he is doing wrong."

The district attorney said that neither the youth council nor Father Groppi was violating any laws. It was not the first, nor the last, time that the priest and his young people would be bitterly criticized for doing something perfectly legal. And it was neither the first nor the last time that the archbishop would defend Father Groppi.

Because the picketing of the Eagles club had provoked almost no response, the youth council decided in August, 1966, to change its tactics and train its marching guns on one man — Circuit Judge Robert C. Cannon. Judge Cannon, a member of the club, was selected as the target because he had a liberal record on civil rights and Father Groppi and the youth council felt that he would cave in more quickly than, say, County Judge Christ T. Seraphim. (Seraphim, too, was picketed later, along with Representative Zablocki.)

From an academic standpoint, the picketing of Judge Cannon's home in Wauwatosa, an upper-middle class suburb immediately west of Milwaukee, involved a classic three-way confrontation of rights: 1) the youth council's right to protest and picket, 2) the judge's right to associate with others in a private club, and 3) the judge's — and his neighbors' — right to peace and tranquility in his own home.

The academics of the situation were completely lost on most Wauwatosans, however. They saw only that their quiet "bedroom suburb" of the tree lined streets and stately homes was being invaded by a group of black slum children. Why the youth council was picketing mattered little to the average resident. Again, as it had so many times in the past in Milwaukee and other cities, the demonstrations and the demonstrators themselves became the issue. The public, instead of focusing on the issue itself, focused on the dramatization of the issue.

For a small but hardy band of white bigots, the demonstrations at Judge Cannon's home were intolerable. Mingling with spectators at the scene, they brought violence to what had been peaceful demonstrations. They tossed eggs, bottles, bricks, and the powerful brand of firecrakers known as cherry bombs, and shouted jeers at the marchers. Some samples: "Go back to the zoo, nigger!" and "Niggers, go back to the jungle!" And, at police: "Nigger lovers!" and "White trash."

Judge Cannon did not cave in as the youth council had expected. He remained adamant about maintaining his membership in the club, although he said he did not agree with the restrictive membership policy and would work for its removal. So the youth council continued its demonstrations.

After about a week, it began to resemble a carnival. The youth council would arrive on the St. Boniface school bus, driven by Father Groppi. White spectators would either be waiting or would arrive shortly after. The crowd was always well salted with goons. Off to the side, a concessionaire sold popcorn, soft drinks, and candy bars from one of those neon lighted white trucks with windows in the sides.

Wauwatosa police and Milwaukee county deputy sheriffs were hard pressed to handle the crowds. Finally, after nine straight nights of demonstrations and increasing violence by white spectators, Wauwatosa Mayor Ervin A. Meier asked for national guard troops to protect the youth council demonstrators.

Four hundred guardsmen were on duty the first night. There were nearly 500 the next night. By Tuesday, August 30, the national guard commander found he could handle the situation with 100 men. But by the time he had learned that, the troops no longer were needed. The civil rights protest of the youth council shifted from the streets in Wauwatosa to meeting rooms.

A lot of people began to get into the act, including a group of clergymen; Joseph C. Fagan, chariman of the Wisconsin Industrial

Commission (later renamed the State Department of Industry, Labor and Human Relations), who conducted hearings into discriminatory policies of private clubs; the State attorney general, Bronson C. La Follette; the Milwaukee Commission on Community Relations (which, as usual, wound up not accomplishing anything), and Nathan P. Feinsinger, a University of Wisconsin law professor who had established a reputation as a top labor negotiator.

After 11 nights of picketing in Wauwatosa, the youth council suspended its demonstrations to meet with a group of about 50 Catholic, Protestant, and Jewish clergymen at Wauwatosa Methodist Church. The clergymen did their best to try to listen to a group of about 10 youth members, although a few could not resist the temptation to lecture them.

What upset the NAACP youth members most was that they were led to believe the clergymen wanted somehow to help them. It soon became apparent at the meeting that most of them wanted the youth council to stop marching in Wauwatosa.

But the clergymen did agree to adopt a statement saying they looked with disfavor on any public official belonging to a segregated club. And they appointed a committee to meet with Judge Cannon and urge him to reconsider his decision not to resign from the club. Nothing came of it, however.

The youth council won one victory. Probate Judge Michael T. Sullivan resigned from the Eagles club. His resignation was more significant because he based it on legal, not moral, grounds. In a written brief stating his reasons for resigning, Judge Sullivan said it was his considered opinion that membership in a segregated club was inconsistent with his oath of office.

On the other hand, there was Circuit Judge Robert W. Hansen (later elected a Wisconsin supreme court justice), who said that if he had to choose, he would rather be an Eagle than a judge. He had been a leading Eagle for many years, and once had served as national president.

La Follette worked behind the scenes with the youth council leaders and their attorney, Thomas M. Jacobson. First the attorney general tried to establish guidelines to limit picketing in Wauwatosa. The youth council rejected them as infringements on their constitutional rights.

Then came the mediation attempt. It was something new in the civil rights movement. Feinsinger, who had ironed out many knotty labor difficulties, offered to smooth out the dispute between the Eagles club and the youth council. It was a fine idea, and Feinsinger did manage to get the issue up to the highest levels in both the NAACP and the Eagles' national organization. But it fizzled.

Early in October, Father Groppi announced that the youth council had organized a commando unit, a direct action force of Negro youths who would handle "very tense situations." The new youth council commandos even had distinctive uniforms — army fatigues, boots, and black berets. (Later they would switch to lettered sweatshirts because most of the commandos could not afford to buy uniforms). Their main job was to function as policemen, to protect the youth council demonstrators and to keep order on picket lines. But they also would conduct their own demonstrations where a situation was likely to get rough.

Formation of the commando unit was partly a reaction to the bombing of the NAACP office and the attacks on youth council members during the Wauwatosa demonstrations. Father Groppi and the youth council leaders wanted their own people to protect members of the organization, many of them girls and children. But, more importantly, formation of the group was an attempt by Father Groppi to develop leadership ability and self-respect among young black men.

Coupled with the earlier guarding of the Freedom House, it was too much for Milwaukee's white majority. Many were shocked by self-induced images of being attacked by black commandos. Some said Father Groppi was another Hitler, organizing a group of "brown shirt" storm troopers. But it was the majority of whites — a few of whom said the priest and his commandos ought to be jailed or shot — who were more susceptible to a fascist way of thinking than the youth council members, who mostly were trying in their own way to get a piece of the democratic pie. And, of course, there was nothing wrong, legally or otherwise, with forming such a group.

Formation of the commandos also was too much for D. D. Billings of Brigham City, Utah, the national Eagles president. Following the picketing of Cannon's home in Wauwatosa and the homes of Zablocki and Seraphim in Milwaukee, Feinsinger had extracted a promise of a demonstration moratorium from the youth council, during which time he promised to work on mediating the dispute. Eventually, Feinsinger managed to set up a meeting between Billings and Roy Wilkins, executive director of the NAACP, in New York city. Father Groppi and several youth council members planned to attend the meeting.

Billings, in telegrams to Wilkins, said he would meet with national NAACP officials, but would not meet with members of the youth council or its commandos. In addition, he said he would not meet with national NAACP officials unless they disowned the commandos. Wilkins replied: "You call upon me as national executive director of the NAACP to 'disown' our Milwaukee youth unit. . . . I cannot do this. Our Milwaukee youth unit is not violating any of the general programs set forth by the NAACP. Although its methods may strike some persons as being unorthodox, the situation to which it addresses itself in 1966, namely, a racial expulsion clause in the membership of, of all groups, a fraternal society, is also extraordinary for this day in this nation."

The mediation efforts failed, and the status quo remained. Father Groppi and some of the youth council members felt they had been betrayed. They had suspended demonstrations in the hope that mediation might produce some sort of a victory. There was no victory, except in the sense that a civil rights organization in Milwaukee had once again pointed out an inequity. However, as a result of the dramatization of the issue, the Eagles club did lose some business. The Milwaukee County Labor Council, for example, honored an early picket line at the club and later decided to discontinue holding monthly meetings there because of the discriminatory membership policy.

It seems to be characteristic of civil rights protests that, once the heat is off, all those individuals and groups that popped up in alarm just fold back into the woodwork, never to be heard from again. The situation with the Eagles club was no different in early 1968 than it had been in 1966 when the youth council started its protest. The hearings, meetings, and discussions of the moment produced little, and there was little followup.

Although Father Groppi said that the youth council planned to keep the pressure on the Eagles club, he also said that he felt the point had been made. The issue evaporated from public view, while the priest and his youth council members discussed their next campaign.

Even before the Eagles club demonstrations ended, Father Groppi had announced that housing would be the youth council's next campaign. In the months that followed, youth council members picketed absentee owners of ghetto properties to call attention to the rundown housing in which many Negroes lived. But the big demonstrations did not start until after the youth council's research committee recommended a campaign for an open housing law in the city of Milwaukee.

As noted earlier, few Milwaukee Negroes lived outside of the area generally known as the inner core. The Wisconsin legislature had passed a state open housing law, which went into effect in December, 1965. However, it was a weak law, which covered roughly 25 percent of the housing in the state, and perhaps as high as one-third of the housing in Milwaukee.

The law applied primarily to the sale and rental of housing where it was a business. Not covered under the law were single family homes and duplexes of four or fewer units in which the owner lived, owner occupied rooming houses with four or fewer roomers, and extra homes or cottages on small Milwaukee lots.

Open housing ordinances had been introduced into the Milwaukee common council four times by Mrs. Vel R. Phillips, who held the dual distinction of being the only woman and the only Negro on the council. Her proposals — the first was in March, 1962 — were virtually ignored. Each time they reached the council floor for a vote, Mrs. Phillips wound up casting the only "aye" vote.

Mrs. Phillips, 43, an attorney and the wife of an attorney, had never been accused of being a civil rights activist. She had participated in a few civil rights demonstrations, but preferred to concentrate on a legislative role. As a result, the tiny woman with the soft voice and sharp tongue was something less than popular with her fellow aldermen. She also had irritated the mayor by criticizing him on civil rights matters.

When the youth council took hold of the open housing issue, Mrs. Phillips became more of an activist than she ever had been. She marched, she spoke at rallies, she was arrested. She even was made an honorary youth council commando — the only woman ever accorded the honor — and was proud of it. "I can't fight the good fight as an alderman and be on hand for every demonstration," she said. "But there are times — if you believe in the right of protest and demonstration and open occupancy — that you have to show this. . . . There are times when you have to participate. You can't really believe it until you do it."

The open housing issue was a natural for the youth council. Lack of an open housing law had helped produce the ghetto, with which most of the youth council members had first-hand experience. And the issue could be easily dramatized because 18 of Milwaukee's 19 aldermen had laid themselves wide open by turning down open housing laws four times. This was particularly true of the half dozen or so white aldermen who had black constituents.

The youth council's first target, on June 19, 1967, was Martin E. Schreiber, alderman and president of the common council, whose ward lay partly in the inner core. Employing their tactic of the previous summer, the youth council members, led by Father Groppi and the commandos, marched from St. Boniface Catholic Church to Schreiber's home in one of the better inner core neighborhoods.

The march attracted attention for several reasons: it was the first civil rights demonstration of what promised to be a "long, hot summer"; the youth council was resorting to the tactic — picketing homes — that had led to much tension and violence the previous summer; and Schreiber was the number 2 ranking elected official in the city.

There was a new twist to the demonstrations. Instead of simply picketing Schreiber's home and letting him wait to hear on radio or television what it was all about, the youth council president, Frederick D. Bronson, and several commandos confronted Schreiber directly. They rang his doorbell and, after Schreiber invited them inside, demanded to know why he had voted against the open housing ordinances, particularly in view of the fact that he had Negro constituents.

A somewhat nervous Schreiber explained that he had voted against Mrs. Phillips's proposals because the state already had an open housing law. He had said earlier, however, that he believed the ordinances proposed by Mrs. Phillips had been fair, and the youth council members reminded him of it. But the common council president refused to say what he would do if another ordinance came up for a vote.

His answers, as might be expected, did not satisfy the youth council members. Bronson promised to march all over the city all summer to get a city open housing ordinance.

During the next four weeks, the youth council picketed the homes of five other aldermen, all of whom had Negro constituents. James E. Maslowski, an alderman who made his living selling real estate, also had his office picketed. The demonstrations had not yet attracted national attention, but top NAACP officials were aware of them. On July 13, Father Groppi and the youth council won the two top national awards from the NAACP for youth council activities. Father Groppi's award was for being the most effective adviser in any youth council in the country; the youth council itself was cited for "the most distinguished service in the fight for freedom."

But Milwaukee's aldermen were not impressed. Whenever an alderman answered the door for the delegation of Bronson and the commandos, the questions — and the arguments — were the same. In most cases, the answers also were the same.

The aldermen earlier had asked for an opinion on whether the city could legally pass an open housing law. City Attorney John Fleming served up the answer the aldermen wanted: No. The reason, he said, was that the state had pre-empted the open housing law field by passing the state law. On the other hand, there was an opinion by the state attorney general, La Follette, which not only said that municipalities could pass their own open housing laws, but added that the state law itself advocated passage of local laws, even those stronger than the state law.

Anyone who has had even a slight brush with the legal profession knows that lawyers can issue opinions on both sides of almost anything. The American judicial system is based on the adversary method.

The aldermen knew this, of course. They had, on past occasions involving other issues, voted against recommendations by the city attorney's office. They knew, too, that they could pass a law that was contrary to the state law — indeed, could even pass an unconstitutional law — and then wait for it to be challenged in court. So the city attorney's opinion, in reality, was nothing more than that — an opinion, not binding on anyone.

But it became the dogma of resistance to open housing ordinances for the majority of the aldermen. When youth council members picketed aldermen's homes and questioned them about their votes against the proposed ordinances, the answer more often than not was that the city could not pass an open housing law because the city attorney had said it could not.

Alderman Robert J. Dwyer, however, had a different approach. He told the youth council leaders that he was strongly in favor of open housing. But, he said, he did not believe in laws to accomplish it. Dwyer said he believed the only way open housing could be achieved would be through some sort of voluntary effort. He also advanced the opinion that most Negroes wanted to live together anyway.

The youth council's demonstrations were peaceful, though often noisy. Sullen crowds gathered during a few of the demonstrations and police and reporters were worried that an incident might break out. One nearly did.

After picketing the home of Alderman Eugene L. Woehrer one night, the youth council members decided to take a stroll around the neighborhood. They had done this without incident in other neighborhoods, but Woehrer lived in a transitional area right on the edge of the inner core where the majority of people were working class whites. Often, in this type of neighborhood, hostility against Negroes is higher than even in some suburbs, mostly because the "threat" is closer.

During the walk around the neighborhood, youth council leaders and commandos good naturedly asked residents if they would rent or sell their homes to Negroes. They also stopped several times to "serenade" residents with civil rights songs.

It was during one such songfest that the situation almost went out of control. A man and a youth were sitting on a short flight of concrete steps leading from the sidewalk up a small hill to the side door of a corner house. The marchers stopped to sing "We Shall Overcome." Only a few feet of space separated the man on the steps from the crowd of marchers on the sidewalk.

He was furious. He shouted several times at the marchers to stay off his grass, although none of them had done any more than poke a toe off the sidewalk. Suddenly, mouthing an obscenity, the man kicked out with his foot. The bottom of his shoe hit a small Negro girl in the chest.

Half a dozen commandos surged through the crowd and were on the man and the youth in seconds. There was a brief scuffle and a few punches were thrown before police could get through the crowd to break it up.

The incident infuriated the commandos, who gathered on a nearby street corner. Most of them wanted to go back and wipe up the sidewalk with the two whites. But they would have had to get past the police first. That made no difference to them, but Father Groppi finally managed to talk the commandos out of taking any further action. However, a white patrolman — unlucky enough to be stationed on the corner where the commandos had gathered — took an avalanche of verbal abuse, fortunately without losing his cool.

That was as close as any of the early summer demonstrations came to violence. Then the riot hit Detroit.

Detroit worried everyone, including some of the youth council members who, along with many other Negroes and whites, were concerned that the same thing might happen in Milwaukee. There were no open housing demonstrations in Milwaukee while newspapers and television were filled with the scenes of destruction out of the Motor City.

Milwaukee was next. And, because of Mayor Maier's tight curfew, hardly anything moved for ten days. It should be noted that the only arrests of any youth council members during the state of emergency were for curfew violations. None were arrested for participating in any way in the riot.

Following the end of the state of emergency, the youth council lay dormant for several weeks, during which time the testimonial dinner for Father Groppi was held. But then it was time to get back to the business at hand.

The youth council wanted to do something dramatically different to focus attention on the open housing issue. The decision was to stage a symbolic march to the south side of the city, followed by a rally in one of the parks there.

The march would be symbolic in the sense that the marchers planned to cross the river valley. Milwaukee's north and south sides were divided by the Menomonee River Valley, which runs from Lake Michigan to beyond the west city limits. The east end of the valley was an industrial area of factories, huge coal piles, railroad yards, and ship loading and unloading equipment.

The city's downtown area lay directly north of the valley. A few blocks north of the downtown area was the south boundary of the inner core, where most of the city's Negroes lived. The south side of the valley was composed mostly of homes occupied by lower and middle income whites, many of whom were factory workers. A small area on the southeast side had become Milwaukee's ghetto for the Spanish-speaking. Spanning the valley were four long bridges — called viaducts by Milwaukeeans — at Sixth, Sixteenth, Twenty-Seventh, and Thirty-Fifth Streets.

The two predominant ethnic groups in Milwaukee, besides Negroes, were the Germans and the Polish. Most of the Germans had been assimilated into the population; in other words, there was no area in the city in 1967 that one could point to and say it was a German neighborhood. However, most of the people of Polish extraction remained on the south side. Yet even so, not even half of the people living there were Polish extraction. The estimated population of the south side was about 350,000, of which some 100,000 to 150,000 were Polish-Americans. Most of them were Catholic.

A reasonably accurate stereotype of Milwaukee's south side would be that it was an area with a high percentage of home ownership, populated by people who worked hard, earned moderately, saved a lot and spent little. In its older sections, many of the streets were physically similar to streets in the inner core. South Sixteenth Street, for example, did not look much different in 1967 than North Third Street, where the July riot broke out. However, the south side neighborhoods generally were somewhat better than those in the inner core, due partly to the high percentage of people who owned their own homes.

The south side also was an area of high resistance to the civil rights movement and, in particular, to Father Groppi. Governor Wallace of Alabama, during his 1964 campaign for the presidency, received some of his warmest welcomes on Milwaukee's south side.

The youth council would get a warm welcome, too — but of another kind. On Monday, August 28, youth council leaders applied for a permit to hold a rally in Kosciuszko Park in the heart of the near south side. The park was named for Tadeusz Kosciuszko, an American Revolutionary war general. County park commission officials refused the permit because, they said, rallies were not permitted in that park. The county had four parks in which rallies were permitted and Kosciuszko Park was not one of them.

So the youth council leaders applied for and received a picnic permit for an area in the park. Park officials emphasized that the permit allowed no speeches, singing or demonstrations. Permit systems for parks, of the sort in effect in Milwaukee county, had been upheld numerous times by the United States Supreme Court as not restrictive of the First Amendment right of assembly as long as they were not used to discriminate against any organizations or groups.

With the picnic permit in hand, youth council members and supporters gathered at the north end of the Sixteenth Street viaduct at 6:25 p.m. the evening of August 28 and started marching to the south side. No one expected trouble. There were only eight policemen guarding the demonstrators, who walked on the west sidewalk.

Among the marchers was a delegation from St. Veronica's Catholic Church on the south side, where Father Groppi had once served as an assistant pastor. Several of them carried a sign: "We South Siders Welcome Negroes."

The route from the north end of the viaduct to the park covered nearly three miles. During the march, the atmosphere was tense but relatively orderly. One scuffle broke out when a heavy set white man tried to block the sidewalk and tangled with several commandos. Police broke it up.

Spectators, many of them teen-agers and children, followed the marchers on the opposite sidewalk. Some of them taunted the marchers. About 40 boys on bicycles trailed behind the marchers.

There were thousands of whites — police estimated the total number at about 5,000 — waiting on sidewalks and street corners in an area of several blocks around the park. Some were unruly toward the marchers and even toward reporters covering the event. One of them kicked me as I walked on the sidewalk among the spectators.

Police cordoned off a small, grassy area inside the picnic spot for which the youth council had a permit and the marchers walked into it. As the white spectators surged around the band of 200 demonstrators, Father Groppi climbed on a picnic table and started talking.

A roar of shouts and boos went up from the mass of spectators, several of whom held up a Confederate flag. Marchers shouted back at the spectators and cheered Father Groppi. The racket made any kind of conversation, even if shouted, impossible.

As the priest held up signs saying, "Fair Housing," "Black Power," and the one about south siders welcoming Negroes, a district park supervisor shouted at Father Groppi through a battery-powered megaphone that he was not allowed to make speeches. The priest said he would comply with the conditions of the permit if police would clear spectators out of the youth council's picnic area. "When you enforce the law on them," he said, "you can enforce it on us."

He also shouted into the outstretched microphones of radio and television newsmen. The governor, he said, called out national guard troops during Milwaukee's riot, and he should do the same thing to protect the demonstrators from the white spectators. Then, in a statement that might have sounded childish under any other circumstances, Father Groppi said: "We're coming back tomorrow night. We want our picnic area."

The demonstrators were in the park only about 15 minutes before they started out to retrace their steps to the north side across the viaduct, which Father Groppi referred to as Milwaukee's "Mason-Dixon line."

Police tried to steer the marchers back onto the sidewalk, but the press of the white mob made it impossible. They surged against the policemen and the marchers, shouting and screaming, forcing the policemen to move the marchers into the middle of the street. There the marchers were surrounded by police patrol wagons and helmeted policemen on foot— by that time, reinforcements had arrived, bringing the total number of police to about 125. All of them were dressed in riot gear.

Traffic stood still as police guided the marchers around automobiles occupied by curious and frightened people. The white spectators, in the wake of the marchers, flowed around the cars. Bottles and stones flew out of the crowds. A Negro woman marcher toppled to the street as a piece of wood thudded into the back of her neck.

When the marchers got out of the area of the park, the crowd thinned. But a hard core mob of about 600 white youths still trailed along, shouting obscenities and chanting, "We want slaves" and "Get yourself a nigger."

A few of them composed new words to a popular Milwaukee polka. The words spread, and soon most of the youths were singing, "Eee-yi-eee-yi-eee-yi-oh; Father Groppi's got to go." In future months, the song would be sung with those same words at wedding receptions on the south side.

It became apparent during the march that the issue, as far as the spectators were concerned, was Father Groppi himself. All along the march route, spectators strained to see him, pointed him out to others, and spat their vilest epithets at him personally. "Nigger lover" was one of the milder ones. Another was, "Why don't you go to confession? You white nigger bastard!" Adjectives derived from four letter words were common.

Police, concentrating on maintaining a tight cordon around the marchers, were forced to ignore the clamor and the occasional stones that flew from the mob. Finally, they held the spectators back and managed to move the marchers back on the sidewalk.

But there was yet another obstacle of hatred to be hurdled. A few blocks from the safety of the viaduct, at a used car lot with the appropriate name of Crazy Jim's, a group of white youths shoved an old Packard hearse across the sidewalk in front of the marchers. The hearse had been painted white. On the side facing the marchers were the words, in black letters: "Last Ride Groppi's" and "White Power."

Police shoved the ambulance aside. But it was not the last time that Crazy Jim's car lot would be the headquarters for hatred.

More stones and bottles flew as the demonstrators walked the last block to the viaduct. Police, some of whom by this time were armed with tear gas guns, moved quickly. One policeman coolly and efficiently ran up to the crowd of white youths and shoved his tear gas gun under their noses. Most of them broke and ran, but one did not get the message quickly enough. The officer grabbed him, whacked him on the head several times with the barrel of the tear gas gun, and propelled him to a patrol wagon.

It was almost like the climax of a movie melodrama. As police fought off the attacking mobs of whites, the marchers half walked, half trotted to the safety of the viaduct. Once on the bridge, they could relax because police were able to effectively seal off the south end. There was no possible way for the spectators to get at the marchers once they started to cross.

At a press conference the next morning, Father Groppi made it quite clear that the youth council intended to stick to its plan to march to the south side again that night, and to take precisely the same route. Whether such an announcement was wise is questionable, but reporters and the public were anxious to know. Besides, the first march had produced a classic confrontation of the sort which had been used effectively in the past by the Rev. Martin Luther King, Jr., to dramatize civil rights issues.

Mayor Maier's reaction was to urge Milwaukeeans to observe a voluntary curfew during the second march — a move that would prove about as effective as tossing a pingpong ball at a charging rhinoceros. In a statement, the mayor also said: "The best thing that can be said about Father Groppi's marches on the south side is that he thinks they will dramatize the civil rights movement. If that is the case, the people of Milwaukee should let the marchers demonstrate in orderly and peaceful fashion. Nothing can be gained by hurling epithets or brickbats. The worst thing that can be said about these marches is that Father Groppi is looking for noise and adulation, along with the national attention that he thinks will result from it. In that instance, the people of Milwaukee will only advance his unworthy cause by allowing themselves to be used for this purpose."

The city was faced with the incongruity of a mayor who asked for a voluntary expression of restraint, while at the same time sanctioning the white mobs by judging the marches — and, by implication, the open housing issue — to be an "unworthy cause."

What the mayor should have done — what he might have done if the situation were reversed — was to issue a statement saying that he would tolerate no violence in the city by anyone, that the marchers had a constitutional right to demonstrate for their cause, and that every measure would be taken to protect the demonstrators and punish those guilty of attacking them.

But he chose not to. His reaction was an old, often repeated refrain for the civil rights movement, which says that if those people would just stop stirring things up there would be no problems. The difficulty with that line of thinking is that little would have been done about the problems of Negroes in the United States if the civil rights movement had not stirred people up. An open housing law in Milwaukee is no less important than a federal law that guarantees Negroes in Selma the right to vote.

With the stage so set, about 200 youth council members and supporters, including some whites and several clergymen, gathered again at the north end of the viaduct for their second foray across the Menomonee River valley. It was a warm Tuesday evening, August 29. This time, everyone was expecting trouble. The marchers were surrounded by 30 uniformed policemen — with more in reserve — 11 squad cars, three motorcycle policemen, and reporters and television crews from the three major networks.

This time, the hoodlums were organized and waiting. Several hundred of them gathered at Crazy Jim's used car lot. Rock 'n' roll music blared from loudspeakers. A grotesque effigy of Father Groppi, with swastikas painted on it, swung by its neck from a rope. There also was a crude, six foot tall caricature of the priest painted on a board. Several youths held up a Confederate flag, while others waved signs saying, "Groppi — Black God," "Trained Nigger," and "Work Don't March."

Police, fearing the worst, rushed ahead of the marchers to cover the used car lot. Newsmen watched tensely. But, except for shouts, jeers, and obscenities, the marchers passed without incident.

Angry spectators lined the sidewalk opposite the marchers but, surprisingly, there was little activity. Half a dozen firecrackers and a few eggs flew from the white crowds, but all they accomplished was to prod police commanders into issuing shotguns and rifles to the policemen guarding the marchers. The marchers picked their way along the sidewalk, guarded by the police on the street side, and by their own youth council commandos, who stood between the marchers and spectators in doorways on the other side.

Then, a few blocks west of Kosciuszko Park, the tightrope snapped. A convertible, bearing signs identifying it as being from Crazy Jim's used car lot, passed slowly by the marchers from the east, its frame members nearly scraping the pavement because of the load of more than a dozen white youths piled into it. They held the effigy of Father Groppi and the signs they had displayed earlier. The crowds cheered.

Moments later — almost as if on a signal — a mob of whites surged into the intersection a block away to the east and rushed toward the open housing marchers. At least a thousand persons were in the white mass, and by the time police realized what was happening, it already was too late to stop them. The mob swarmed around the police and the marchers, who were huddled against buildings on the north sidewalk behind commandos. The commandos had stepped forward to face the attack.

Some of the whites rocked a squad car while others tossed eggs and other debris at Father Groppi and the other demonstrators. There was pandemonium — a riot by any definition.

The police recovered quickly. A group armed with shotguns pointed their weapons at the sky and fired them as fast as they could pump fresh shells into the chambers. The fusillade startled the crowd as, almost simultaneously, other policemen tossed or shot tear gas bombs into the mob.

The whites scattered and police quickly moved the marchers off onto a side street. Police wanted the marchers to turn back, but Father Groppi said: "We won't move out of our shell. We'll stay here until the National Guard comes and we can march like free American citizens." Someone started singing, "Ain't Gonna Let Nobody Turn Me Around," a song that had been sung in many southern civil rights demonstrations — and the others joined in.

When the police realized that the marchers were determined to continue, they surrounded them and marched them quickly down the middle of the street to the park. The marchers sat on the grass in a cordoned off area and Father Groppi complimented them. "You've shown you're willing to die for freedom," he said. He also asked them not to hate the white mobs. "Feel sorry for them," he said.

The priest never completed his next sentence. As he was saying "Jesus Christ died for brotherhood . . ." a firecracker went off in the midst of the marchers, injuring a Negro man, a Negro woman, and a white woman. The firecracker blew a woman's purse apart. It never was determined whether it had been tossed by a spectator or dropped by a marcher.

Immediately after the explosion, the marchers, surrounded by policemen, left the park at a fast walk — almost a trot. Again whites trailed along, tossing bottles, eggs, and rocks. But the situation was not nearly as serious as it had been earlier — that is, not until the marchers passed Crazy Jim's used car lot again.

The white youths had gathered again at the car lot, waving their signs and flaunting the effigy. As the marchers passed by, scores of bottles flew from the crowd of whites and rained down on the marchers, newsmen, and police. They started running down the street as other policemen fired tear gas shells into the lot.

By the time the marchers reached the safety of the viaduct, they looked like refugees from a battle. They were dazed and bewildered, some still suffering from the effects of tear gas that had hung in the air. Some could not walk and had to be carried by other marchers. Blood streamed down the face of a young white seminarian who had been hit by a bottle. Others had assorted cuts, bumps, and bruises.

In one of his rare tributes to the police, Father Groppi commented that he thought they had done as good a job protecting the marchers as was possible under the circumstances. He repeated his contention that they needed the help of national guard troops.

When the marchers finally reached the north end of the viaduct, and the youth council members boarded the St. Boniface school bus, it looked as if peace had been restored to Milwaukee. But the night was not yet over.

Father Groppi and the youth council members returned to their Freedom House on North Fifteenth Street, then fled from it when a fire started. It was a complete loss. The earlier tribute to the police was soon forgotten; the youth council members and Father Groppi said police had started the fire with an unprovoked tear gas shell fired into the house, then kept firemen away until it was too late to save it. The police said a fire bomb was tossed into the house — one said he saw a car speed away — and they could not let the fire trucks in because there was a sniper in the area. Youth council members said the gunshots came from police weapons. No arsonist or sniper ever was found.

Mayor Maier's reaction was to ban night marches and demonstrations. In a proclamation issued the next morning, the mayor prohibited "marches, parades, demonstrations or other similar activities . . . upon all public highways, sidewalks, streets, alleys, parks and all other public ways and public grounds within the city of Milwaukee between the hours of 4 p.m. and 9 a.m."

Some Milwaukeeans raised the question of whether the proclamation was an unconstitutional infringement on the open housing advocates' right of assembly. The mayor replied that the proclamation was designed to protect freedom of assembly. He even said that anyone who wanted to participate in a peaceful assembly after 4 p.m. could do so. But he said, "We're going to hamstring the kind of mobility that existed before this, to preserve the public peace."

The explanations of the proclamation were fuzzy and even seemingly contradictory. The city attorney, John Fleming, said that the ban on night marches and demonstrations applied uniformly to all such activities (a necessary ingredient to save the proclamation in a court test). But then he said it was up to the police on the scene to determine whether whatever was happening was a peaceful assembly (which was okay) or a demonstration (which was not). The United States Supreme Court has not shown a great deal of sympathy toward too much police discretion in situations involving First Amendment rights.

There were other constitutional questions, such as whether violence on the part of spectators was sufficient justification to limit the First Amendment rights of the marchers. But as far as the youth council members and some other Milwaukeeans were concerned, the proclamation was aimed at one thing and one thing only — to keep the open housing demonstrators from marching.

Nevertheless, there was some confusion among the youth council leaders. So instead of a third night of marching, open housing supporters gathered, at Father Groppi's invitation, for a rally at the burned out Freedom House on Wednesday night, August 30. The reasoning was that the house was on private property, which was not subject to the mayor's proclamation.

There were several hundred persons in the crowd, among them Mrs. Vel R. Phillips, Milwaukee's Negro alderman. The crowd was too large for the Freedom House property. Young people leaned out charred windows, others stood on the rickety porch, in a vacant lot next door, and on debris in the tiny front yard. But many also spilled out onto the sidewalk and in the street. Father Groppi had not arrived.

Prentice McKinney, one of the youth council commandos, began to introduce Mrs. Phillips. As he was talking, police wearing helmets and carrying riot sticks formed ranks at a nearby intersection and marched toward the crowd. A police captain, using a battery powered megaphone, shouted at the crowd to disperse. He also read the mayor's proclamation. While he was talking, policemen moved in and scattered the crowd. Some demonstrators were stubborn. They were promptly arrested and taken to waiting patrol wagons. The police chased small groups of demonstrators several blocks.

Mrs. Phillips was furious. After running with the others, she stood on a corner, watching, and demanded of no one in particular: "What the hell is going on? This is absolutely unbelievable. . . . They had a right to have a rally. I thought we'd be able to have a peaceful meeting."

Then came a scene that would have fitted into a Keystone Kops comedy. As policemen chased demonstrators all over the area, Father Groppi appeared with about 30 other persons at the intersection where Mrs. Phillips was standing and calmly walked to the Freedom House. The group was not even challenged.

Policemen returning from their dispersal activities found themselves facing a group of people in the same area they had cleared a few minutes before. The policemen stood in the street and watched quietly. Demonstrators, some of whom had scattered earlier when the police moved in, boldly returned to the Freedom House singly, in pairs, and in small groups. Father Groppi said, "The rent's paid," and told everyone to gather on the property. And, in characteristic Groppi fashion, he shouted at the police: "Why didn't you tell the people here to get on the property instead of beating those ladies with clubs?"

The group rapidly swelled to about 150 persons, all of them crammed on the porch and in the small, littered area in front of the house. The situation soon turned into something not unlike a children's game, with the demonstrators saying in effect, "I dare you," and the police looking for an excuse to respond to the dare. The demonstrators sang "We Shall Not Be Moved" and "Ain't Gonna Let Nobody Turn Me Around," and chanted "We hate coppers,"

"We hate Maier," and "Get off the north side, cops."

In the street, the police watched closely. Every time a demonstrator stepped out on the sidewalk, several policemen would rush in and arrest the person. Men and women were picked off in this fashion. After about a half hour of the see-saw game, police moved all of the newsmen away from the house to a nearby intersection. The intersection would provide no vantage point at all, so another *Journal* reporter and I sneaked to the porch of a nearby vacant house, from which we could view the whole scene.

Twenty minutes later, the police formed into ranks and rushed at the crowd. "Let's go clean out the house," one shouted. "They're under arrest, every one of them." But the actions of individual policemen varied. While some grabbed demonstrators, arrested them, and rushed them off to patrol wagons, others simply moved people away from the house. In the confusion, Father Groppi and several commandos went through the Freedom House and slipped out the back door. He returned to St. Boniface Church, picked up the school bus, and drove back to the area, hoping to pick up stragglers. But police had cordoned off the area and would not let him in.

A deputy police inspector explained that he decided to declare the crowd an unlawful assembly because the singing and shouting was disturbing the peace. But taken as a whole, the police action that night did seem at least somewhat inconsistent. A veteran police reporter commented at the time that he thought perhaps there had been a mixup in communications. First the police broke up the crowd, then permitted it to gather again, and then broke it up a second time.

The reporter also commented that it seemed as if the police were returning to a get tough policy with civil rights demonstrators. I was under the same impression. Milwaukee's policemen had gained a lot of experience with civil rights demonstrations in 1965 and 1966. In the summer of 1967, they had displayed an admirable amount of coolness in dealing with civil rights demonstrations, avoiding anything that might provoke an incident. But the attitude seemed to change that night at the Freedom House.

In defense of the police, it must be pointed out that they were under tremendous pressure. They were caught right in the middle. Even south side whites now were accusing them of brutality, a charge heretofore made mostly in Milwaukee's Negro ghetto.

A total of 58 persons were arrested in and around the Freedom House that night. Meanwhile, Milwaukee Archbishop William E.

Cousins had called for "Christian thinking" on the part of white hecklers and "Christian prudence" on the part of the demonstrators.

Earlier in the day, Paul J. Moynihan, a Milwaukee advertising man who was chairman of the city Commission on Community Relations, had met with the archbishop on Mayor Maier's orders. The purpose of the meeting was to persuade the archbishop to limit Father Groppi's civil rights activities. This he refused to do. Instead, Archbishop Cousins called on public officials, businessmen, citizens, and religious and civic organizations to work together for immediate action on the causes of unrest in the community. Future violence, he said, had to be avoided at all costs.

But it was not to be so. Youth council members and their supporters, convinced that their constitutional rights were being violated, laid plans to deliberately violate the mayor's proclamation. The issue had switched briefly from open housing to freedom of assembly. More than 400 persons, among them nuns and clergymen, crowded into St. Boniface Church Thursday night, August 31, and listened to Father Groppi denounce the mayor and his proclamation. Mrs. Phillips was among those at the rally. Youth council commandos hoisted her on their shoulders, to the cheers of the crowd.

Nearly all of those in the church shouted their assent when Father Groppi asked if they were willing to march, and nearly all of them did march. But the march, headed toward city hall to protest the proclamation, went only four blocks before police moved in and arrested 137 of the demonstrators, including Father Groppi and Mrs. Phillips. Nearly six months later, the priest was convicted of resisting the officer who arrested him. During the confusion of the arrests, a television cameraman was slugged on the head with a riot stick wielded by a policeman.

The next day, Friday, Mayor Maier announced that the emergency proclamation banning night demonstrations and marches would be lifted as of 9 a.m. Saturday, September 2. Originally the proclamation was to have been in force 30 days. It lasted three. The proclamation had accomplished its purpose, the mayor said.

But this minor victory did not stop the youth council. The nation had focused on Milwaukee. Roy Wilkins, executive director of the NAACP, had sent Mayor Maier a telegram saying he was "outraged over the failure of (the) city of Milwaukee to protect (the) constitutional rights of NAACP youth council members." Supporters poured into St. Boniface Church for the Friday night rally.

The youth council had momentum and was not about to trip itself up.

More than 500 clapped and sang at the rally, which started in the church and later moved onto the St. Boniface School playground. The rally lasted four and one-half hours, while youth council attorneys sought court orders to prevent police from enforcing the mayor's proclamation — even though the proclamation was scheduled to be lifted in less than 12 hours.

When the attorneys did not succeed, Father Groppi and the youth council leaders decided to march anyway. It had become a stubborn matter of principle. More than 400 demonstrators lined up and marched out of the playground. The lead marchers — Father Groppi and Sydney Finley, a field director for the NAACP from Chicago who had arrived earlier — walked perhaps a hundred feet before police stopped them.

Policemen grabbed Father Groppi first. The rest of the marchers broke ranks and crowded onto the lawn of North Division High School, which adjoins the St. Boniface playground. Contrary to a standing order of the youth council leaders, some of the marchers had armed themselves with bottles and cans. Several threw them at police in the street. Finley and the commandos quieted the crowd and the marchers formed ranks again, did an about face, and started marching back the way they had come. More bottles and a few rocks flew from their ranks toward the police. The marchers turned up an alley and walked back onto the playground.

They massed in a driveway leading into the playground, facing a line of policemen in the street. For five minutes, it looked like a standoff. A bottle and a rock flew from the crowd of marchers, but the police held their ground.

A moment later, a marcher near the front lobbed a pop bottle at one of the policemen. The officer ducked, then ran into the crowd to grab the thrower. Other policemen followed him in single file. They looked like football players coming out of a huddle.

The marchers scattered around the playground. Police fired tear gas shells in every direction. Three of them landed at the back door of the rectory. Others fell near the convent. (Firemen later were called to ventilate parish buildings.) The playground was covered with tear gas fog. Policemen also fired tear gas at a crowd of spectators who gathered at an intersection a block away.

Most of the marchers eventually found their way to the St.

Boniface hall in the basement of the church. In a postmortem, some shouted angrily for retaliation, while others angrily criticized those who had tossed the rocks and bottles. The demonstrators were ready to march again when they learned that Father Groppi was out on bail and on his way back to the church. There was no more marching that night. The priest announced that the youth council was seeking support of national civil rights leaders. One would respond, as he always did: Comedian Dick Gregory.

There was one serious casuality that night. Tolbert Harris, Jr., a 64-year-old Negro and former army captain, collapsed and died of a heart attack during the abortive march. Mouth to mouth resuscitation efforts by a white woman marcher and a white policeman were fruitless.

Gregory arrived Saturday, the day the proclamation was lifted, and support for the youth council snowballed. More than 1,000 persons, some of whom had never been in a civil rights demonstration in their lives, participated in a triumphal though uneventful 16 mile march to city hall and through the south side that Saturday night. Marches continued over the Labor Day weekend and daily after that.

Milwaukee, in the words of some out of towners, became the "Selma of the north." Sympathizers poured into the city to march with the youth council, particularly on weekends. Among them were many white clergymen, who viewed the demonstrations as the last hope in the nation for the preservation of integration and nonviolence in the civil rights movement. If the youth council could win a victory in Milwaukee, they reasoned, it would help discredit the antiwhite black nationalists who had been arguing for separatism and against nonviolence.

Indeed, St. Boniface Church began to resemble Brown's Chapel during the Selma demonstrations. Every out of town supporter checked in at the church hall. Tables were set up to direct people to housing. Donations of food and money poured in A room was set apart for a first aid station, manned by a white doctor and other volunteers. Sweatshirts and tee shirts sold as fast as the youth council could order them. The shirts carried the words "Milwaukee NAACP Youth Council" on the front and slogans on the back. Among them were "Sock It to Me Black Power," "Black and Beautiful," "I Love Father Groppi," "Remember McKissick" (the youth who had been shot by a policeman following the riot), "Soul

Sister" and "Soul Brother" (for white supporters), and "Rats."

The youth council was riding high. It had the attention of the country, and Father Groppi had achieved national stature as a civil rights leader. They could, in part, thank the mayor for it. His proclamation banning night marches and demonstrations contributed to it and cost him some of the prestige he had earned in so skillfully squelching Milwaukee's riot a month before. Negroes and whites in Milwaukee who had never before been seen in civil rights demonstrations arrived at St. Boniface to participate in the marches. Some white liberals who had abandoned the civil rights movement for protests against the Vietnam war returned to march in what, in late summer 1967, was an old fashioned civil rights protest.

Then came one of those unpredictable events that cost the youth council some of its increasing support. On September 7, a group of youth council members and other teen-agers, led by commandos, went to Mayor Maier's office to conduct a sit-in. Contrary to plans, the sit-in got completely out of hand.

In a display of uncontrolled, out and out vandalism, the young people tore up the mayor's outer office. They slashed chairs, defaced furniture, overturned file cabinets, and left the office a shambles. It was a setback for the youth council and a victory of sorts for the mayor, who now had ammunition to charge that Milwaukee's civil rights movement was populated by hoodlums.

Father Groppi, as might be expected, would not apologize for the incident. His response was that black people in Milwaukee and elsewhere had more of a right to be violent than any other group of people in history. Nevertheless, the youth council commandos suspended two of their own members for three days for permitting the sit-in to get out of control.

Events after the first march to the south side had a somewhat sobering effect on the commandos. Where before they had been a boisterous, somewhat loosely knit, and often disorganized group, the south side marches and subsequent events brought about a new cohesiveness — what the commandos referred to as being "up tight." Enforcement of the rules became stricter — for example, as in a military academy, any commando who observed misconduct on the part of another commando was required to report it to the rest of the members at one of the daily meetings.

The organization also was having the effect Father Groppi probably had hoped for when he organized it ten months earlier. There was a new respect for the black male in Milwaukee's Negro community. Hardly a day went by in the early weeks after the south side marches that young Negroes did not come to St. Boniface seeking to join the commandos. There were no artificial requirements for, or barriers to, membership. It did not matter where a man lived, or whether he had been in jail, or whether he was working, or at what kind of job, or even, for that matter, whether his skin was black. About the only thing prospective members were asked was whether they were on probation or parole, and what the probation or parole officer's reaction might be to the man joining the commandos.

Once in, the rules were simple. The main job was to protect the marchers. A commando had to be on call any hour of the day or night, and had to be willing to fight and die for the cause. Objectively speaking, death was a remote possibility. But most of the commandos themselves considered it extremely likely — and, in their minds, it probably would be at the hand of a policeman. The memory of Clifford McKissick was still on the minds of many Negroes in the inner core. Some of them, including the commandos, were convinced he had been murdered, the justifiable homicide ruling notwithstanding.

Other commando duties included guarding St. Boniface and making certain there was no drinking or profanity on the premises. For a group of tough young ghetto men, some with criminal records, there was a surprising amount of respect for the church building. One night a commando leader bodily ejected a prospective commando after he mouthed an obscenity in a basement rest room, then said another obscenity when the commando leader told him not to use foul language in the church building.

Later there was a minor leadership struggle within the organization over the fact that a few of the leaders were not as dependable about attending meetings and doing their marching duties as some of the lower echelon men. The top leadership changed, and the organization became even tighter than before. Haircuts were required; "do jobs" or "conks" (processed hair) were forbidden and the commandos were organized into squads so every man was responsible to someone who, in turn, was responsible to the top leaders. The organization used a ranking system similar to that of the army.

Among the top leaders after the shakeup were Richard E. Green, two star general (the highest rank), one of eight children of a Milwaukee family and a member of St. Boniface Church; Henry L. Walters, brigadier general, father of three girls and an ex-paratrooper; James Pierce, colonel, a high school dropout from a family with ten children; and Milton C. Latson, major, a highly vocal young man who had served a prison sentence for severely beating a policeman with a piece of fishing pole.

There were others, most of them basically good young men. Sometimes their behavior might not fit into a white country club setting (although they could adapt to that, too), but they had no split level homes in suburbia in their backgrounds either. And, although many of the commandos had been in trouble with the law before joining the organization, the only scrapes with the police after joining had to do with civil rights protests.

The commandos were advocates of Black Power, in the sense of black self-determination. Their rhetoric frequently was antiwhite, yet they welcomed white supporters, even to conferring honorary commando status on 75-year-old Ignatius W. O'Connor, an Irish Catholic bachelor from Boston who never missed a march. O'Connor, a pleasant old man with a ready laugh, fell in love with the commandos and the youth council members, and the commandos respected his dedication to their cause.

Commandos emphasized that they were not nonviolent, that the nonviolent demonstrations they were conducting were a tactic, nothing more. They said they would retaliate if attacked or if it became necessary to defend an open housing marcher from attack. Many were arrested during the open housing demonstrations.

The open housing marches reached a peak three days after the incident in the mayor's office. Supporters traveled to Milwaukee from all over the country. More than 2,300 persons walked 15 miles in the march on September 10. The commandos had great difficulty keeping the mass of people orderly, even with assistance from young black men from out of town. Even so, they probably would have succeeded if there had been no rest stop halfway through the march. At the rest stop, on federal grounds named Wood, Wisconsin, near a veterans administration hospital, the mass of people changed from a long line of marchers to a large crowd.

A fight broke out between a commando and a white spectator as the commandos tried to funnel the crowd back into a line of march. Many of those in the crowd ran to see what was happening and, for a

few minutes, there was mass confusion. Again, a few of the marchers
had ignored the warnings of Dick Gregory and top commandos and
had armed themselves with empty soft drink bottles and other
missiles. A few were tossed at houses in the neighborhood, marring
what otherwise had been an orderly march. Then, on the way back,
some of the marchers smashed store windows as they passed.

Still, considering the poor communications that exist in a march
that large, along with the fact that the youth council and the commandos had no control over who participated, the march was
remarkably orderly.

Meanwhile in those early September days, the anger at Father
Groppi and the Negroes of the youth council among Milwaukee's south
siders jelled and a new organization was born — the Milwaukee Citizens for Closed Housing. It was a loosely knit group of whites whose
primary interest at the time was in getting rid of Father Groppi. The
group organized counter-demonstrations and marches, several of
them to the Milwaukee archdiocesan chancery office in an attempt
to get Archbishop Cousins to transfer or discipline the priest.

The "forced open housing" opponents, as they called themselves,
soon had their own "Father Groppi." Father Russell F. Witon, a white
priest who was chaplain of a hospital in the city of Port Washington
30 miles from Milwaukee, came to the city to join the "forced open
housing" opponents. Curiously, Father Witon had a background
very similar to Father Groppi's. He had lived in the same neighborhood and had attended the same grade school and high school as
Father Groppi, although the two men apparently did not know
each other.

Father Witon's stated purpose was to oppose Father Groppi's
"means and methods." But although he tried to present a moderate
image, some of his public statements fed the fears of his new flock.
After leading a march through the inner core one night — a march
that resulted in a near clash with open housing supporters who also
were marching — Father Witon told his group: "We are not going
to let those savages — those black beasts — take our rights away."
He said that the whites had to fight not only the black man, but the
Catholic church and clergymen who supported open housing as well.
"It is the very devil that is behind these people," he said, "and we
have to pray for their souls."

After its initial stridency, the "forced open housing" group settled
down somewhat and made efforts to present a more moderate and

responsible image. Members even started saying that thy did not really oppose open housing, just open housing laws. The name was changed to fit the new image, and the organization became the Milwaukee Citizens Civic Voice.

In this period, Archbishop Cousins was being subjected to sustained and often vituperative pressure to do something about Father Groppi, such as excommunicate him. In response, the archbishop spoke directly to the nearly 700,000 Catholics in the ten county Milwaukee archdiocese on September 16 through a medium he had not used before — the editorial columns of the *Catholic Herald Citizen,* the weekly archdiocesan newspaper. In the opening paragraphs, Archbishop Cousins referred back to his major civil rights address of August 6 — apparently many Catholics already had forgotten it — and then went right to the point. He wrote:

Now to the immediate demands that Father Groppi "be defrocked" — "have his collar torn off" — "be suspended" — "be sent back to Africa" — etc. etc.

Is this the answer? Do you honestly believe that Father Groppi's absence from the scene would somehow miraculously heal all wounds and cure all our social ills? If the decision were that simple do you suppose that no one else would have thought of it?

Some of my correspondents called me "stupid," "blind," "weak," "cowardly." Let me make one thing clear — any course of action in important matters, and far-reaching decision is arrived at only after long and frequent consultation with many whose knowledge and judgment and common sense are above dispute. You might disagree with their recommendations but they are possessed of facts and information that are vitally important in reaching logical conclusions.

If Father Groppi were out of the picture, the NAACP youth council would not go out of existence. Its direct action committee would continue to determine tactics. Its large legal staff would still advise. The parent organization would maintain its present position and lend its support. More to the point, the underlying causes of unrest pointed up by the youth council would go on plaguing us. They existed long before Father Groppi's advent.

Unfortunately, Father Groppi has become an issue in himself. People are so disturbed by his actions that they lose sight of the cause for which he is fighting — that of freedom and human dignity. As Christians we favor the same just cause, but many are being sidetracked into a hate campaign directed against one man. That campaign is being aided and abetted by forces that are failing in their own responsibilities by "passing the buck." The Church is being split into factions while the real problems go unsolved. We are being diverted by emotion and mob psychology into fighting a straw figure while the real enemy goes unscathed.

Some have gone so far as to "leave the church." If disagreement with the tactics and conduct of a priest could justify such action, the Church of Christ would never have come into being. Peter denied the Master, Judas betrayed Him and the Apostles forsook him on the night preceding His death. If the acceptance of Christ's teachings depended upon the perfection of His followers we would be in a sad way. We would not sacrifice our American heritage because a high government official, in our judgment, fell into apparent disrepute.

Others have withdrawn or have threatened to withdraw financial support from the Charity and Development Campaign, from local parishes, indeed from all church causes. Here again in their resentment of a particular priest they are striking out in all directions.

Even if the priest is wrong, he is not being punished by action that hurts innocent parties like the poor who have in no way been involved. Speaking facetiously, this action resembles that of a man who has a violent argument with his wife and then goes downstairs and kicks the dog.

The archbishop said he did not agree with everything that Father Groppi had said and done, any more than some of the Catholics to whom he was speaking. "However," he said, "the real and basic issues should be the name of the game. Name calling accomplishes nothing."

In his editorial, the archbishop pointed up a chronic problem that had afflicted the Milwaukee civil rights movement from the beginning. This was the almost instinctive reflex among most Milwaukeeans of making issues out of symptoms, of focusing on the dramatization of the issues and the personalities involved instead of the issues themselves. First it had been John Givens and members of the Milwaukee CORE chapter, then Lloyd A. Barbee and the Milwaukee United School Integration Committee; now it was Father Groppi and the youth council.

But not all Milwaukeeans suffered from emotionalism and gut reaction. In the city and suburbs, a wave of support began building for passage of open housing laws. Scores of responsible organizations and groups came out in support of open housing. Among them were church and civic groups, labor and business organizations, newspapers and television and radio stations. Even the Committee of We — Milwaukeeans, which represented the "white power structure" and the city's moderate Negro leadership, issued a statement supporting open housing laws for Milwaukee and all its suburbs.

The sense of urgency was heightened by sporadic incidents involving open housing demonstrators. The most serious occurred on Sunday, October 8. Open housing marchers were returning to St. Boniface Church after a peaceful two-hour walk through the north side when commandos learned that members of the Milwaukee Citizens Civic Voice had arrived in the city's inner core on a march from the south side.

The commandos hastily organized a second march to go out and confront the south siders. It turned into a chase. Police tried to steer the south siders away from the youth council marchers, but they took shortcuts, walked rapidly, and sometimes even ran to catch up. The two groups converged at an intersection and walked along opposite sides of the street with police and newsmen in between. At an intersection with a traffic light, the commandos attempted to lead their group across the street to intercept the south siders, but police stopped them because they would have been walking against the light. At the next intersection, the youth council marchers had the green light and again tried to cross.

A dozen policemen with riot sticks moved in front of the marchers and shoved them back. Those in front had difficulty moving because of the press of the marchers behind them. The policemen started swinging their riot sticks, clubbing those in the front ranks. The marchers broke ranks and milled around a grassy area at the intersection, while other policemen escorted the south siders away from the area.

Angry commandos lined up facing the policemen while youth council members chanted, "Eight fingers, two thumbs; send those cops to Vietnam." After a few minutes, the commandos reorganized the march and headed back toward St. Boniface. They had gone only a few blocks when Father Groppi and Dick Gregory arrived.

The two men conferred with the commandos and rounded up those who had been injured, while the marchers stood still and taunted the policemen who stood across the street. The police held back, although one of the demonstrators tossed a rock that hit a squad car. A policeman in the car jumped out, ready to toss a tear gas grenade. Gregory ran across the street and shouted angrily at the policemen, while commandos circulated through the crowd of marchers, yelling at them not to throw anything.

The police lieutenant in charge, using a portable loudspeaker, asked three times to speak to march leaders, but was ignored. With the situation becoming increasingly tense, the police decided to exercise discretion — they pulled out of the area, apparently hoping the marchers would walk back to St. Boniface.

But their hopes proved fruitless. The demonstrators, angry over what they considered to be the unnecessary force used earlier by the police, turned to civil disobedience. Instead of marching back to St. Boniface on the sidewalk, they formed ranks and headed toward the south side — but this time they were walking in the middle of the street. They went five blocks with police nowhere in sight. Fortunately, it was a Sunday night and there was no traffic on the street, a major artery through the inner core.

It was 10 p.m. when the squad cars drove up behind the band of about 200 marchers. The police lieutenant warned them three times that they were violating the law, but the demonstrators paid no heed. It was clear that they planned to provoke arrests.

Squad cars speeded ahead, trucks loaded with reserve policemen arrived, and the police formed ranks at an intersection half a block ahead of the marchers. Commandos, walking slowly, blocked other squad cars and several policemen got out of the cars to clear the marchers away. Gregory, his hands in his pockets, pushed up against the policemen and was shoved back several times. When he continued, a policeman arrested him. He was led away to a patrol wagon.

A few minutes later, the policemen who had formed ranks at the intersection walked up to the group of demonstrators, who by this time had stopped in the street, waiting. The lieutenant in charge again told the marchers three times that they were violating the law and asked them to move out of the street. When they did not, he asked if any wanted to submit to arrest voluntarily. No one moved.

The policemen waded into the crowd and the demonstrators scattered. Some marchers resisted when they were arrested and were hit with riot sticks. One Negro youth fell to the street as a policeman was shoving him toward a patrol wagon. The policeman slugged the youth repeatedly with his riot stick until the youth was screaming for mercy. Then he hit the young man several times again as he was shoving him into the wagon.

Father Groppi slipped away in the confusion. Most of the demonstrators straggled back to St. Boniface in small groups. The score for the evening was 13 arrested and more than 40 injured.

The following night, Monday, October 9, youth council commandos again provoked police action by marching around an inner core intersection. Police again broke up the march and arrested eleven persons. Twenty-seven, including six policemen, were injured.

Efforts to get the city government to take action on an open housing law stepped up, but Milwaukee's 18 white alderman did not budge. Nor did the mayor. His position was that a city open housing law would increase the flight of whites from Milwaukee and eventually would result in what he called an apartheid society. The mayor's position was consistent with one he had taken three years earlier, when he advocated passage of open housing laws, but on a metropolitan or state-wide basis. He did modify his stand somewhat during the open housing demonstrations by saying he would back a city law covering all housing. But the law would go into effect only after 14 of 27 Milwaukee suburbs also passed similar laws.

Milwaukee's aldermen, creatures of a ward system of government, knew exactly which side they had to be on. Elections were less than five months off and the aldermen sensed political suicide if they supported any kind of open housing law.

Finally, the common council's judiciary committee scheduled a public hearing. Six hundred persons jammed into the common council chambers to watch 25 persons testify for passage of an open housing law and 11 persons testify against it. The hearing was mostly a vocal exercise. It changed none of the aldermen's minds.

But there was one hopeful result. Ben Barkin, a public relations counsel and a leading Milwaukee citizen, made an impassioned plea for the establishment of a special government-citizen committee to hammer out some sort of compromise. Barkin, a devoted civil rights advocate, was convinced that the city was on the verge of an explosion. He had been working quietly behind the scenes to try to maintain lines of communication between members of the white power structure and the youth council and Father Groppi.

Barkin was in a curious situation. He was the leading advocate for the youth council and its cause among Milwaukee's civic and business leaders. Yet the youth council, as part of its open housing campaign, was urging a boycott of the product made by one of Barkin's major public relations clients — Schlitz beer. What made it even more incongruous was the fact that the Jos. Schlitz Brewing Co. was a leading force for civic betterment and had, in fact, contributed money to civil rights causes and programs to alleviate the problems of Milwaukee's black ghetto.

The Schlitz boycott happened somewhat by accident. It was

touched off by Dick Gregory, who suggested in speeches at St. Boniface various ways of putting economic pressure on the city to get passage of an open housing law. Gregory, not familiar with the city or the background of the situation, probably selected Schlitz beer because it symbolized the city — "the beer that made Milwaukee famous" — and because it may have been the first thing that popped into his mind.

It was typical of Gregory's talent for making things happen in the civil rights movement. Although he had no organization and no following one could point to, he commanded enormous respect in the Negro community and had an ability to influence events. The youth council's subsequent Black Christmas campaign, in which Milwaukee's Negroes were urged to boycott Christmas shopping and traditional Christmas decorations, also was an idea that originated with Gregory.

To the surprise of many, Barkin's suggestion for a citizen-alderman committee to hammer out an open housing compromise found favor with the common council judiciary committee. But it was to be another exercise in futility. The special committee, composed of five aldermen and six representatives of citizen organizations — including the youth council — came out of a 19-hour session in a hotel room with four open housing proposals, ranging from a law that would cover all housing to one that would duplicate the Wisconsin state open housing law.

It appeared that some sort of action would be taken by the common council. But on the city's south side, the opposition had been busy. The day before the common council was to meet for a vote, representatives of the Milwaukee Citizens Civic Voice walked into city hall with nearly 27,000 signatures on a petition. The petition directed the common council to order a referendum on a question that, if passed, would have prevented the council from enacting any open housing law for two years.

The signatures on the petition were certified in a matter of hours, faster than was usually the case, and the council later ordered the referendum. But the Milwaukee chapter of the American Civil Liberties Union, smelling a victory because of recent United States Supreme Court decisions in the open housing area, filed suit in the federal district court in Milwaukee to block the referendum on constitutional grounds.

Meanwhile, the youth council continued its daily marches and open housing advocates in the city and suburbs redoubled their efforts. The efforts started bearing fruit. Bayside, a tiny "bedroom suburb" village in the string of suburbs north of Milwaukee, became the first community in the Milwaukee area to pass an open housing law.

There were scoffers, particularly in Milwaukee's city hall. It made no difference, they said, because no Negroes could buy homes in the suburb anyway. It was hypocritical, they said. There was some truth to the charges. The belief that the law would not make any difference was a strong factor in persuading the members of the Bayside village board to vote for the law. But it was significant, nonetheless — the first law in the area to affirm the right to housing regardless of race, religion, or national origin. And it did represent a victory for Father Groppi and the youth council members who had raised the issue and kept it in the public eye.

In the months to come, other suburban communities followed suit. By April, 1968, twelve Milwaukee suburbs had passed open housing laws. With one exception — Wauwatosa — all the laws were stronger than the existing state law. The Wauwatosa law was an exact duplicate of the state law. Four other cities within commuting distance of Milwaukee — Port Washington, Oconomowoc, Racine, and Waukesha — also passed open housing laws. Prior to the youth council's campaign, the only communities in the state that had open housing, laws were Beloit and the state capital, Madison.

Milwaukee passed an open housing law, too, but it accomplished little. On December 12, after weeks of debate, bickering, negotiations, and behind the scenes buttonholing, the Milwaukee common council met and approved an ordinance that exactly duplicated the provisions of the state law. The only difference was that it provided for local enforcement through complaints to the city attorney's office — a less cumbersome procedure than that in the state law, which required investigation, mediation, conciliation, and hearings that could eat up more than a year of time from complaint to disposition. The Milwaukee law went into effect three days before Christmas, 1967.

Father Groppi referred to the common council's action as "tokenism and crumbs." Alderman Phillips, who had made four attempts during the council meeting to amend the law and make it stronger, said: "Thanks for nothing. You are very much too late with very much too little."

The youth council vowed to continue marching — for five years if necessary, according to Father Groppi — to get a stronger city law. The council also continued its Black Christmas campaign — a tactic that sharply divided Milwaukee's Negro community. Black Christmas was directed at getting Negroes to completely boycott the commercial aspects of Christmas by not putting up Christmas decorations or buying Christmas gifts. The idea was originally Gregory's. He said he had boycotted Christmas once, saved $8,000 by doing so, and had been boycotting Christmas ever since. The purpose of the campaign was to put economic pressure on the city's business community in the hopes that businessmen, in turn, would exert enough pressure on city hall to force passage of an open housing law.

Black Christmas was highly successful in the sense that it kept the inner core area bleak for the holidays. While on a typical Christmas, many inner core homes would have been elaborately decorated and lighted, only a few lights and no extensive decorations graced ghetto homes for Christmas, 1967. But the lack of decorations indicated fear as well as support of the youth council. Many Negroes were bitter over Black Christmas, but feared retaliation if they decorated their homes. A lot of the celebrating of Christmas was done covertly.

Downtown business suffered, but whether the Black Christmas campaign could be held responsible was a question. More likely, business was down because most of the Milwaukee area's white shoppers believed that it was not safe to go downtown. It mattered little that the downtown was no less safe than it had been six months earlier — before the riot, open housing demonstrations and Black Christmas. What counted was that people believed it was not safe.

There were a few incidents of vandalism in the inner core, but none could be traced to the youth council or the commandos. The incidents appeared to be the work of teen-agers who apparently used the Black Christmas campaign as an excuse for attempts to terrorize some homeowners. Police received many complaints of threats, but did not come up with any evidence against any youth council member.

In the early months of 1968, attention focused on the referendum and Federal Judge Robert E. Tehan, whose job it was to decide the Civil Liberties Union suit to block the referendum. Open housing supporters viewed the possibility of a referendum with a great deal of apprehension, believing that it would further deepen the split between Milwaukee's Negro and white communities. They also were convinced that extremists of various persuasions would come to Milwaukee in the weeks before the referendum to urge or argue against its passage. In that event, there might have been nasty confrontations that again might focus unfavorable attention on the city.

But their fears were never realized. On March 4, in an historic decision with implications for cities all over the country, Judge Tehan ruled that the referendum could not be held.

"The resolution which is presented to us in this case would be patently unconstitutional if enacted into law," the judge wrote in his opinion. "No good reason has been shown for its submission to the electorate. On the other hand, considerable evidence has been presented which convinces the court that the holding of the referendum would do great irreparable injury not only to the plaintiff and his class but to the city as a whole. Under these circumstances submission of the resolution to the electorate must be enjoined."

The plaintiff in the case was James T. Otey, a Negro who worked as a community center worker for the Inner City Development Project, an antipoverty agency in Milwaukee.

There had been little defense by the city against the suit. An assistant city attorney merely argued that the common council had acted according to state law in placing the referendum question on the ballot. The city did not argue the constitutionality of the referendum resolution.

"Without question," Judge Tehan wrote, "the record reveals that the resolution is intended to and, if passed, will secure to those desirous of discriminating in the area of housing their 'right' so to do for a period of two years at least." In addition, he said that "the record contains uncontroverted testimony that if the resolution is enacted into law, the common council will abide by it by refusing to consider any open housing legislation while it remains on the books. Council members would be happy to consider themselves bound by this expression of the will of the people, constitutional or not, and refuse to act."

A representative of the Milwaukee Citizens Civic Voice, the organization which gathered the petition signatures for the referendum, testified at the trial that his organization favored open housing at levels of government other than the city. Judge Tehan viewed it differently.

"A study of the testimony," he wrote, ". . . reveals quite clearly that the MCCV wants no open housing legislation at all, that its protestations of wanting such legislation on a broader level are an obvious sham, and that the group was organized to move to block the possibility of open housing wherever it reared its head. It is opposed to local open housing legislation now because that is the type of open housing legislation being considered. When broader legislation is considered which will encompass local housing, we are certain the MCCV will be equally opposed, just as it is opposed to the weak state law now in effect. The court rejects as incredible (the) declaration that MCCV members, who have done nothing thus far but oppose open housing, were inspired by the August marches to the south side and their violent reactions to band together to try to secure open housing on any level."

The resolution on the referendum, Judge Tehan ruled, would if passed violate the rights to equal protection of the laws guaranteed to Otey and other Milwaukee Negroes under the Fourteenth Amendment of the United States Constitution.

Seventeen days later, the Milwaukee NAACP youth council and Father Groppi marched together again and then suspended the daily marches. Demonstrations, in the form of marches and rallies, had continued for 200 consecutive days since that first tense walk to Kosciuszko Park on August 28, 1967. Some youth council members and supporters added extras when they marched again on succeeding nights. But the official end was at 200.

They had not won the victory they set out to win, but there was a reasonably good box score. Open housing laws now existed in 17 communities where there had been none before.

In the Spring of 1968, Milwaukeeans waited to see what the youth council would do next. And they also looked forward — with some trepidation — to what the summer would produce for the city of beer, bratwurst, and gemütlichkeit.

IX

CITY WITH A CHANCE

In late 1967, when the national eye had swung away from Milwaukee even though the commandos and other members of the Milwaukee NAACP youth council continued daily marches for an open housing law, a lonely hand-written sign hung on a basement wall in St. Boniface Catholic Church. Aside from the people who gathered in the basement, the sign was the only reminder of the hectic days there when the open housing marches were at their peak. And, although the youth council did not win the victory it sought, that sign symbolized the fact that even though Milwaukee had not listened, it still was a city with a chance. The sign read:

U		D
N		I
I		V
T	Black Power	I
E		D
D	$+$	E
		D
W	White Power	
E		W
	$=$	E
S		
T	Community	F
A	Power	A
N		L
D		L

137

The sign illustrated a basic fact about the people in the civil rights movement in Milwaukee, and perhaps about the majority of black people everywhere, that in spite of the frustration, the rejection, the discrimination, and the suffering, they were still willing to give white society a chance. The young people of the youth council and the commandos, at least, were still willing. They had not yet, as so many of the brothers and sisters had in other cities, chosen the path of black separatism. That they had not chosen to close the door on white society was more realistic but less understandable than if they had gone the way of the separatists. Frederick D. Bronson, the soft-spoken, articulate president of the youth council, described the attitude when he said: "We're not antiwhite; we're just pro-black. We defined black power for ourselves some time ago. To us, it means a struggle for political and economic unity and self-determination for the black man. But blacks cannot reach full economic strength alone. Whites control the money and the economic strength, and it's going to take white help to bring the black man to equality."

Father Groppi and other white men and women like him, who proved to the black community that they cared, were partly responsible for this attitude. The fact that the militant civil rights movement in Milwaukee was still integrated and basically nonviolent was, of course, totally consistent with the philosophy of the NAACP. But it was not consistent with the thrust of black militancy elsewhere, which had become increasingly antiwhite and disenchanted with nonviolence as a tactic.

There is no way, except with the hindsight of history, to know whether the Milwaukee militants were in a backwater of the civil rights movement or whether they somehow skipped over the bitter antiwhite stage to move forward again toward the more realistic goal of assimilation into the mainstream of American society. The major issues — open housing and de facto school segregation — and the tactics of marches and demonstrations certainly were old-fashioned enough. Militants in other cities no longer cared about nonviolent demonstrations or advocacy of integration into white society. In Detroit, for example, the cry was for better facilities and more black teachers and black principals for the black schools, not elimination of de facto segregation.

The situation was perhaps also an indication of the basic conservatism of most of Milwaukee's citizens, both black and white. Although a strain of bigotry existed among the whites, there also was a degree of moderation. After the white toughs rioted against the open housing marchers on the south side, several representatives of the American Nazi Party traveled to Milwaukee, sensing fertile ground to plant even greater hatred. Yet when the Nazis organized a "white power" march into the inner core, only about a dozen people showed up. The embarrassed Nazis left and were not heard from again. Some Milwaukeeans might be bigoted enough to react violently in a disorganized fashion, but they apparently were not willing to go so far as to put on swastikas to support organized hatred.

In the black community, the basic moderation showed in the posture of the civil rights organizations. Even the small and relatively uninfluential Milwaukee CORE chapter still was integrated and working nonviolently on programs to get jobs for inner city residents. The national CORE organization, meanwhile, had abandoned the goal of integration and had become increasingly militant and nationalistic.

Nevertheless, the desire for black power existed in Milwaukee in late 1967 and early 1968. Even Father Groppi spoke more of "territorial expansion" than integration on the question of housing. The open housing issue itself was rooted more in a desire for decent housing than any yearning for integration. It was a matter of basic principle — to guarantee black people freedom to find decent housing wherever it might be.

The desire for black self-determination also showed among young people. In early 1968, students at inner core high schools and junior high schools became involved in demonstrations for black history books and more black cooks in school cafeterias. Some even demanded "soul food" in their cafeterias. A few of the demonstrations, unfortunately, resulted in some violence and vandalism, and most Milwaukeeans once again focused their attention on symptoms instead of substance.

Underlying the demands and demonstrations, and even the negative vandalism, was an essentially positive component — a new sense of dignity and pride among the students. No longer were they ashamed of their blackness. Nor did they believe that white necessarily was right. It was a surge of self-respect and a desire for a hand in shaping their own destiny. Some manifestations of this new self-awareness among the students may have been misdirected, but misdirection is nothing new among blacks or whites, young or old, in the United States.

Such restlessness and dissatisfaction can lead to alienation or ambition, depending on the reaction. In Milwaukee, there were hopeful signs that at least some people in power were reading the situation accurately. Under a new schools superintendent, Richard P. Gousha, school officials were exhibiting more willingness to respond to grievances of parents and students. Gousha personally met with student demonstrators who demanded more Negro history books.

Other public officials, particularly state officials, also were making efforts in late 1967 and early 1968 to solve the problems of Milwaukee's inner core. As a first step, the Wisconsin legislature allocated $4.75 million for special programs, most of them for inner core schools. But more important, the people who would be affected by the programs were given a voice in how the money was spent.

Chief among the public officials active in the inner core was Joseph C. Fagan, chairman of the Wisconsin Department of Industry, Labor and Human Relations. Fagan firmly believed in self-determination and involvement for black people in programs that affected them. He developed lines of communication between the state government and inner core residents that never had existed before, and was instrumental in getting other state officials to follow his lead. As a result of his efforts, for example, the NAACP youth council commandos were able to develop and get state money for a program of their own. It was designed to rehabilitate young men coming out of jail or prison.

An indication of the basic reasonableness that existed in Milwaukee's civil rights movement was the fact that the commandos, the most militant civil rights activists in the city, worked closely on the project with the Milwaukee Urban League, an agency considered moderate by most Milwaukeeans. Much of the credit for this was due to Wesley L. Scott, the league's executive director. Scott, though not a militant of the sort who makes headlines, had a deep understanding of the inner core, its people, and its problems.

The city moved, too. After delays and bickering, Mayor Maier finally got the common council to approve a federally financed model cities program for Milwaukee. In its application for funds, the city officially recognized the problems of poverty and discrimination that existed within its boundaries. The mayor also reorganized the Commission on Community Relations so it could get to work on his long awaited "War on Prejudice," part of which included opening offices in poor neighborhoods on the north and south sides of the city. Federal money for a rat control program also came through.

However, communications between city government and inner

core residents were still almost nonexistent in early 1968. But a possible break in the situation came when the mayor appointed as one of his staff assistants the first black man ever to serve as a mayoral assistant in the city's history. In a curious twist of history, the new assistant was none other than John H. Givens, Jr., who as chairman of the Milwaukee CORE chapter in 1963 had led the first civil rights sit-in ever held in the mayor's office. Appointment of a black assistant was one of the promises Mayor Maier had made following the riot in July, 1967. Whether the appointment would have the desired effect of improving communications remained to be seen — the mayor was adept at turning staff members into mirror images of himself.

Givens' appointment came shortly before the April 2, 1968, elections in which Mayor Maier was re-elected to a four-year term in office by the greatest margin any Milwaukee mayor ever had achieved. The mayor swamped a liberal young attorney, David L. Walther, but a vote of 172,156 to 27,936. Walther conducted an issue-oriented, though financially deficient, campaign and advocated strong open housing laws and better police-community relations.

Maier campaigned mostly as an apologist for his view of the progress made in the city during his administration. He also maintained a continuous harangue against *The Milwaukee Journal* and the *Milwaukee Sentinel,* charging that the two newspapers were engaged in an evil conspiracy to upset his agenda for community progress.

Maier won all 19 wards in the city, including the 6th ward of Mrs. Vel R. Phillips in the center of Milwaukee's black ghetto. The vote there was 2,189 for Maier and 2,011 for Walther. But Maier's biggest margins came in south side wards where opposition to open housing legislation was strong. In two of the south side wards, the mayor took 95 percent of the vote.

The mayor's triumph was overshadowed when, two days later, an assassin's bullet killed the Rev. Martin Luther King, Jr., as he stood on a second floor balcony of the Lorraine motel in Memphis, Tennessee. King's death sparked a national outpouring of grief — black and white — that had not been experienced in the nation since the assassination of President John F. Kennedy. But the civil rights leader's violent death also produced violence. Rioting erupted in scores of cities all over the country.

But not in Milwaukee. The city's black community did not translate its grief into burning or looting. It was quiet in the inner city that Thursday night, so quiet that the crime rate was down. "This is a sad community tonight," a white policeman commented. "It was like the day Kennedy was shot."

Father Groppi celebrated a requiem mass for King only hours after the slaying. He told about 150 persons who attended in St. Boniface church: "I know tensions are going to rise in our community. It's not really a question at this time of what we would want to do, it's a question of what Dr. Martin Luther King would want us to do. Dr. King was a nonviolent man. Many of us disagreed with him. . . . (But) at this time we must do what he would want us to do — he being of the nonviolent philosophy, I think this is the honor we owe to him."

Meanwhile, some of the youth council commandos went around to inner city taverns, urging the tavern operators to close out of respect for King.

Milwaukee expressed itself in a way totally consistent with King's philosophy of Christian nonviolence. On the Sunday following the murder, more than 7,000 blacks and whites attended a memorial service organized by Negro clergymen's groups. Mayor Maier was one of the speakers.

Because of the mayor's participation in that memorial service — held in a park outside the inner city — the NAACP youth council and other civil rights and neighborhood organizations boycotted it. They held their own memorial service in Garfield park in the center of the ghetto area. Father Groppi urged those in the crowd — a younger and more militant group than the one that heard the mayor — to continue to be nonviolent. For Father Groppi, it was only one of many times he made the same plea. A few days earlier, when 1,000 students walked out of an inner city high school over King's death, the priest also had urged them to be nonviolent.

On Monday, April 8, Milwaukee experienced the biggest civil rights demonstration in its history when up to 15,000 persons walked through the inner city and the downtown area in a memorial march for King. It also was one of the largest memorial demonstrations held for King anywhere in the country.

Although scores of windows along the march route were broken — most of them by youngsters — businessmen and city and county officials praised the march for its orderliness. The credit had to go to the youth council commandos, who did yeoman duty in policing the march. They kept the ranks dressed, chased youngsters who threw rocks, guarded stores where windows had been broken, and generally maintained order while city police stayed inconspicuously in the background.

Three days later, President Johnson signed the federal open housing law of 1968, which was passed by a congress shocked into action by King's assassination. The next day, Mayor Maier jumped on the bandwagon and announced that he would recommend immediate enactment of a city ordinance modeled after the new federal law.

Maier, snugly settled in a new four-year term in office, even was so brash as to propose that the entire city ordinance go into effect immediately, although the federal law was not to be fully effective for nearly two years. This was the same man who previously had adamantly resisted efforts to have the city strike out on its own in open housing.

But the common council, with seven new members as a result of the April 2 election, provided even more of a surprise on April 30. The aldermen passed an ordinance stronger than the federal law. The new ordinance contained all of the provisions of the federal law, plus an amendment that made the ordinance cover apartment buildings with three or more living units, instead of the five or more in the federal law.

The only exemptions in Milwaukee's new law were owner-occupied rental dwellings with one or two units, and, in sales, owner-occupied single family homes if the owner handled the sale without outside help. Such a sale, moreover, was only exempt if the owner did not have more than three such properties at one time, and only if he did not discriminate in his advertising.

All of Milwaukee's seven new aldermen voted for the new ordinance. Four of six south side aldermen, whose constituencies were nearly 100 percent white, also supported it. But the crucial vote in the passage of the ordinance came from the new common council president, Robert J. Jendusa, who said he hoped the amendment might "heal some of the wounds of the community." Only a few months before, as chairman of the council's judiciary-legislation committee, Jendusa had been a leader of the open housing opposition.

Among about 60 persons who attended the council session were Father Groppi and Lawrence Friend, a young black man who was the new president of the youth council. "We do consider this a significant victory," Father Groppi said. Friend singled out Jendusa. He said he was surprised and gratified by the alderman's understanding of the problem.

Mrs. Vel Phillips, who had tried for six years to get the common council to act on open housing, commented: "The council has given me hope. Maybe the white power structure recognizes the frustrations of the black community."

The movement for open housing continued in the suburbs, too. By July, 1968, a total of 26 other communities in and near the Milwaukee metropolitan area had passed open housing laws. Among them were 16 of the 18 suburbs in Milwaukee county. Six of the 26 communities, including two suburbs on the southwest side of Milwaukee, had laws without exemptions.

On July 16, 1968, the Milwaukee County Board of Supervisors passed an all-inclusive open housing law covering Milwaukee and the 18 suburbs. However, the law would apply in individual communities only after they passed legislation to accept it and to grant the county authority to enforce the new law.

There were other hopeful signs. A million dollars of the special money allocated by the state legislature was earmarked for special inner city projects. The projects, screened by a committee of inner city residents, started taking shape in late spring and early summer.

Meanwhile, the white power structure was becoming more responsive to the black militants. For example, when some of the youth council commandos proposed expanded recreation programs for the inner city, several members of the Committee of We — Milwaukeeans did the arm twisting necessary to persuade school and county park officials to go along with the proposal.

The business and industrial community also began to stir. In a welcome but belated recognition of responsibility, the 2,600 member Metropolitan Milwaukee Association of Commerce committed its resources and staff to Milwaukee's racial and poverty problems. One of its first projects was working with the National Alliance of Businessmen to find summer jobs for young people and permanent jobs for the hard core unemployed.

Yet with all the movement, the problems of poor housing, unemployment, and inferior education in the inner core still existed, as they had for many years. And black hostility toward the police department was as strong as it ever had been.

Milwaukee's police chief, Harold A. Breier, was an honest man, a tough cop who ran his department by the book. The difficulty was that the book was outdated. The city had a fine police department, free of corruption and highly efficient in terms of apprehending criminals. But its image in the inner core, and that of its chief, continued to be that of an oppressor. There were people, as Father Michael Neuberger put it, who still believed that a white policeman could murder a Negro in cold blood and get away with it. Whether the belief was valid is, again, beside the point. The fact that it existed was reason enough for increased efforts at better relations between the police and the black community. Yet Chief Breier showed no inclination toward changing the status quo.

But the biggest problem of all, as in any city, was the white majority. Most whites in Milwaukee and elsewhere reacted to the 1967 and 1968 riots as they often reacted to civil rights demonstrations. The symptoms instead of the disease became the issue. Whites shouted for law and order but failed to realize, as Dick Gregory has often said, that there can be no law and order without justice.

The basic need for the white majority is a massive dose of compensatory education. Most black people know more about whites than whites know about them, so there is little need for education in the black community except in the sense of book learning and skills training. Whites need to know and understand their black fellow citizens. The prejudices and stereotypes run deep, often so deep that whites themselves sometimes are unaware of their existence. There is cause for pessimism in this, particularly because the support of the white majority is necessary for the massive, vastly complicated, and expensive task of bringing about what the United States Advisory Commission on Civil Disorders called "common opportunities for all within a single society." There is no reasonable alternative.

Yet there also is cause for optimism, mostly because of young people who are increasingly better educated and less inclined toward prejudice and discrimination than their parents. This is why integrated education still must be the goal, because white society needs it. It already has started, in the sense that many white children are now exposed to black faces via television and textbooks, whether or not their parents want it. Young people are at least slightly better educated in human relations. But full integration in educational institutions would speed the process.

History is on the side of assimilation of black people into American society. It may be delayed but it will not be denied. Most of the issues raised by the civil rights movement in Milwaukee and elsewhere have been vindicated; the ones that have not been simply need a little more time. Organizations like the Milwaukee Citizens Civic Voice will be viewed by historians as quaint examples of a segment of the population that lived in a dark age although its time period was mid-twentieth century.

But the chief cause for optimism, in Milwaukee at least, was that the majority of its black citizens still persevered, still had not rejected the goal of an integrated, democratic society. In spite of many slaps in the face, they were still willing to work toward that goal with white society. In mid 1968, it was mostly because of them that Milwaukee still was a city with a chance.